SELF-PORTRAIT IN BLACK AND WHITE

ALSO BY
**THOMAS CHATTERTON
WILLIAMS**

Losing My Cool

SELF-PORTRAIT IN BLACK AND WHITE

FAMILY, FATHERHOOD AND RETHINKING RACE

THOMAS CHATTERTON WILLIAMS

JOHN MURRAY

First published in the United States of America in
2019 by W. N. Norton & Company, Inc.
First published in Great Britain in 2020 by JM Originals
An Imprint of John Murray (Publishers)
An Hachette UK company

This paperback edition published in 2021

1

A CIP catalogue record for this title is available from the British Library

Paperback ISBN 9781529372144
eBook ISBN 9781529322858

Book design by Barbara M. Bachman

Printed and bound in Great Britain by Clays Ltd, Elcograf S.p.A.

John Murray policy is to use papers that are natural, renewable and
recyclable products and made from wood grown in sustainable forests.
The logging and manufacturing processes are expected to conform
to the environmental regulations of the country of origin.

John Murray (Publishers)
Carmelite House
50 Victoria Embankment
London EC4Y 0DZ

www.johnmurraypress.co.uk

For

MARLOW AND SAUL,

WHO HAVE TAUGHT ME

NEW WAYS TO SEE.

It was necessary to hold on to the things that mattered.
The dead man mattered, the new life mattered;
blackness and whiteness did not matter;
to believe that they did was to acquiesce in
one's own destruction.
—JAMES BALDWIN, *NOTES OF A NATIVE SON*

Why waste time creating a conscience for
something that doesn't exist?
For, you see, blood and skin do not think!
—RALPH ELLISON, *INVISIBLE MAN*

CONTENTS

AUTHOR'S NOTE

HAVE TRIED TO CAST DOUBT ON AND REJECT TERMS (AND their synonyms) such as "white," "black," "mixed," "biracial," "Asian," "Latino," "monoracial," etc., throughout this text. In so doing, I have frequently placed them in quotation marks. But for comprehensibility's sake, inevitably I also have to fall back on our language's descriptive conventions, identifying people in some instances as they are commonly understood. If I use these terms and do not place them within quotation marks, for example if I mention a black classmate or a white police officer, it is because this is the way these people have defined themselves or been defined. It does not mean that I believe these terms are helpful, accurate, or true.

I have also changed certain names and descriptive details of some characters who could not have been aware that they were interacting with a memoirist during the times that we shared.

SELF-PORTRAIT IN

BLACK AND WHITE

PROLOGUE

N OCTOBER 2013, AFTER A LATE DINNER WITH VISITING American friends, my wife's water broke. In a daze of elation, Valentine and I did what we'd planned for weeks and woke her sister's boyfriend, Steve, who gamely drove us from our apartment in the northern ninth arrondissement of Paris to the *maternité*, all the way on the city's southern edge. At two in the morning, we had the streets practically to ourselves, and the route Steve took—down the hill from our apartment, beneath the greened copper and gold of the opera house, and through the splendor of the Louvre's court-yard, with its pyramids of glass and meticulous gardens, over the Seine, with Notre Dame rising in the distance on one side and the Grand Palais and the Eiffel Tower shim-mering on the other, and down the wide, leafy Boulevards Saint-Germain and Raspail, into Montparnasse, through that neon intersection of cafés right from the pages of *A Moveable Feast*—was unspeakably gorgeous. I am not permanently awake to Paris's beauty or even its strangeness, but that night, watching the city flit by my window, it did strike me that such a place—both glorious and fundamentally not mine—would be my daughter's hometown.

Another twenty-four hours elapsed before Marlow arrived. When Valentine finally went into labor, even I was delirious with fatigue, sustained by raw emotion alone and thinking incoherently at best. On the fourth or fifth push, I caught a snippet of the doctor's rapid-fire French: something, something, something, "*tête dorée* . . ." It took my sluggish mind a moment to register and sort the sounds; and then it hit me that she was looking at *my* daughter's head and reporting back that it was *blond*. The rest is the usual blur. I caught sight of a tray of placenta, heard a brand-new scream, and almost fainted. The nurses whisked away my child, the doctor saw to my wife, and I was left to wander the empty corridor until I found the men's room, where I shut myself and wept like all the other newborns on the floor. I mean newborn literally. Along with the litany of universal realizations—of new and daunting responsibilities, of advancing age—I was aware, too, however vaguely, that whatever personal identity I had previously inhabited, I had now crossed into something new and different. When, finally, I'd washed my face and returned to meet my child, she was having amniotic fluid vacuumed out of her stomach. I sat beside my wife and helplessly watched our baby struggle into existence. Once she was calm and safe, the nurse passed her to us, and she squinted open a pair of inky-blue irises that I knew even then would lighten considerably but never turn brown. For this precious being grasping for milk and breath, I felt the first throb of what has been every minute since the sincerest love I know. And I also felt, if I'm honest, something akin to the fear of death electrify me to the core. *What have you done?* the voice of my superego or something far stricter demanded from some distant region of my mind well beyond conscious control. *What have you done!* I willed it to silence. An hour or so later, when Valentine and the baby were asleep for the night, I fell back into a taxi, my own brown eyes absentmindedly retracing that beautiful and quasi-foreign route.

I HAVE SPENT my whole life earnestly believing the fundamentally American dictum that a single "drop of black blood" *makes* a person "black" primarily because they can never be "white." I say fundamentally American, because elsewhere it is not the same. In Brazil, for example, a drop of "white blood" *makes* someone *not*-black.* Before my daughter, Marlow, was born that night in Paris, I'd never remotely questioned the idea that, when the time came to have them, my children would be "black" like me. They would be mixed, yes, but that's a matter of degree for all of us whose roots

---

* A stunning painting from 1895, *The Redemption of Ham*, depicts the state-subsidized colonial practice of *blanqueamiento*, or "whitening," through the process of compelled marriage between dark-skinned Brazilians and lighter-skinned European immigrants so that traces of Africa might "disappear into the whirlpool of the white race." In the picture, an elderly, dark-skinned grandmother stands to the left of a young mixed-race mother, white father, and white-looking child. Her hands raised, the grandmother praises God. More recently, in 2010, Neymar da Silva Santos Júnior, the brown-skinned, curly-haired soccer superstar who is the son of a black father and white mother, was asked if he had ever experienced racism. "Never. Not in the field, nor outside of it," he famously replied. "It's not like I'm black, you know?"

stretch far enough back—as far as I was concerned, they'd be as black as Frederick Douglass or W. E. B. Du Bois, Lenny Kravitz or Halle Berry. Blackness as an either/or truth was so fundamental to my self-conception that I'd never rigorously reflected on its foundations. My own father, whom we call Pappy in a nod to his Southern roots, is a red-brown man. Despite a dusting of freckles under the eyes and a prominent, in my mother's teasing words, "Indian" nose, no one has ever described him as anything other than black. His appearance, along with the strength of his persona, allowed me to assume that the Williams family identity would forever be in his image, even though my mother is unambiguously white—blond-haired, blue-eyed, and descended on all sides from Northern European Protestant stock.

When my father was my baby's age, there were still horse-drawn buggies and outhouses where he lived. That was in the 1930s in Galveston, Texas, a short sliver of an island in the Gulf of Mexico that bears the deplorable distinction of having been the very last place in the entire United States of America to free its slaves, some two and a half years after Lincoln's Emancipation Proclamation. Never a rich man, Pappy, whose own grandfather was born in the final year of chattel slavery, nonetheless leveraged an education to leapfrog several generations and get us into the kind of middle-class environment my brother and I were able to believe was normal. By the time I was born in 1981 in suburban New Jersey, my father had effectively cut our family off from whatever Southern black roots we might have had. My brother and I were raised in a small but gloriously book-crammed house by loving and devoted parents who came from elsewhere. They kept few photographs or clues to the past and valorized individuality, cultivation, and self-creation over membership in any particular lineage or clan. I did not have the language for it then, but compared to all of my Polish and Italian and Puerto Rican and black and Irish and Catholic neighbors and classmates, what was odd about my parents was just how anti-tribal they seemed. We did not belong to any collectives. My mother is a devout Christian, but her faith was a private matter and it was only after my brother and I left the house that she began attending services again. Though we always went to Catholic schools, as a means of getting us out of our own little town, I realize now, my parents prohibited us from attending mass. Every Tuesday morning when the entire school walked across the street to church, we sat in the lobby with the uncomprehending secretaries, buried in our magazines and books—an early, tremendously difficult, and priceless lesson in developing the habit of standing apart.

We stood apart in the secular realm, too. Pappy is constitutionally allergic to the willed snobbishness of black social organizations like Jack and Jill, just as he and my mother wanted nothing to do with their white equivalents. As a foursome, we were an island unto ourselves in the de facto segregated town whose white side we lived on as a form of silent protest against the insulting attempts of various realtors to steer us across their invisible but all-too-real red lines. Yet, despite these eccentricities, we also never questioned that ours was an unequivocally *black* household. Sometimes my father would even half jest that his wife wasn't really white at all—she was just "light-skinned," he'd say with a laugh. Once, when I was ten or so, I pressed him on this. "Come on," I said. "You don't really believe that, do you?" "Well, she's got black consciousness, doesn't she?" was all he'd say. It strikes me now as an adult that this exchange could occur nowhere else in the world but in the United States, and yet it made a certain amount of sense to me then. What I know is that my parents tried to prepare my brother and me for the reality beyond their doorstep as best they could—by confidently and proudly proclaiming and championing our blackness so that, in turn, we might do the same when the world would inevitably demand that we take a stance.

Beyond that door, however, and from a very young age, it became clear to me that no matter her "consciousness," others would insist on perceiving differences between my mother and me. In my earliest memory of this rift, we were in the checkout line at ShopRite. I must have been four years old, horsing around obnoxiously with my brother. Mom, who was trying hard to count out her cash and coupons in peace, wheeled around and commanded us both to be still. When she finished the scolding, an older white woman who had been watching leaned over and actually said: "It must be so tough adopting those kids from the ghetto."

In the 1980s and for a good portion of the nineties, even in a New Jersey suburb within commuting distance of Manhattan, we were a family that drew sometimes confused, sometimes hostile stares when we ventured out to eat. And though I did know and go to school with a number of "black" children in possession of all manner of skin tones and hair textures, I was unaware of anyone who consciously defined themselves as "biracial" until I arrived at Georgetown University in 1999; there wouldn't even be the option to select more than one race on the national census until the turn of the millennium. Which is simply to say, I am old enough to understand why even many blacks still wax nostalgic for segregated days: there is safety and comfort in easy unity and acceptance, even when that unity is organized around artificial and sometimes contradictory lines.

IN 2012, a year before Valentine got pregnant, I published an essay in the *New York Times* defining my future children as unassailably black. In retrospect I can see it was a defiant last gasp of . . . *something*—some way of looking at the world—that I must have understood, whether I wanted to admit it or not, was under dire threat. At the time, I was convinced I was in the right, and even prevailed on my wife to accept the same view, which was completely foreign to her European mind. Today, I wince when I read that op-ed. Parenthood changes everyone, but looking back on it now, I can say without exaggeration that I walked into the delivery room as one person and came out an altogether different man. The sight of this blond-haired, blue-eyed, impossibly fair-skinned child shocked me—along with the knowledge that she was indubitably *mine*. On some deeply irrational but viscerally persuasive level, I think I feared that, like a modern Oedipus, I'd metaphorically slept with my white mother and killed my black dad.

The reality of Marlow's appearance had rendered my previous "one-drop" stance ridiculous in my own eyes. When I look at my daughter now, I see another facet of myself, I see my own inimitable child. But I also know that most people who meet her will—and will *want* to—call her "white." And I can't help but wonder if I've nudged my family across a threshold, the full consequences of which I may or may not fully discern in my own lifetime.

THE DAY AFTER Marlow was born, Nicolas, my jovial father-in-law, brought me to the nearest town hall to register and name my child. In France, this formality must be completed within the first three days of birth and so in practice remains a paternal prerogative. Nic joked that I might as well avail myself of the opportunity to name her whatever I pleased—did I have any second thoughts? he said with a laugh. I recalled that this was precisely how Steve had ended up *Steve* and not Marc, a fit of creative fancy having overtaken his own father in the *mairie* as his mother recuperated in bed. I understood the temptation. A part of me was seized by the desire to scribble down Jemima—or even Shaniq'wa—on that official blue paper of the République Française. A nominal but glorious middle finger to middle-class black notions of respectability as well as a subversion of any apparent whiteness, an amusing reappropriation—perhaps even *transcendence*—of lingering ethnic stigma. I had half-seriously floated the notion to Valentine when she first got pregnant, and let it go soon after she replied that it was manipulative to the point of irresponsibility. Our baby's coloring, however, had reawakened the desire for rebellion in me. But a child's life is not a sarcastic or even political gesture. I carefully scrawled *Marlow* in the space allotted for *prénom*, just as we'd agreed, and this was itself the somewhat ironic consequence of our mutual love for the HBO series *The Wire*, coupled with a more practical need to find a combination of syllables that would be equally pronounceable in English and in French. Not all French people have middle names, but it seemed necessary to me that Marlow have one and that it carry some ancestral weight. So I also wrote down *Cora* in tribute to my father's beloved grandmother, a member of the first generation of her line to be born into emancipation. It would later be impressed on me that Cora is the name of a chain of big-box stores in France, and that to most French people's ears it sounds like "Walmart." This would be my first, though not my last, lesson in the incommunicability of meaning and significance between the various realities that Marlow will have to straddle.

VALENTINE SPENT a generous six days and nights in a private room courtesy of the French state before we bundled our baby in blankets and brought her home. I had put some thought into what ought to be the first song she would ever listen to in that inaugural ride—that first parental stab at cultural indoctrination—and finally settled on "Mushaboom" by Feist. *And we'll collect the moments one by one*, her soft voice flitted around the car. *I guess that's how the future's done.* It is by no means a black song, and that had caused me some anxiety, too. There was that internal voice again. *What's wrong with some Stevie Wonder, man?* But anxiety is only a fraction of what I felt. Every moment with Marlow rendered the nagging questions and the silly terrors more and more beside the point.

"Aw, son," Pappy said, chuckling while cradling Marlow in his arms for the first time when he and my mother visited a few weeks later. "She's just a *palomino*!" There was—there still is—something so comforting to me in his brand of assurance. It's certainly true that in his day and in his fading Texas lexicon, black people could be unflappable when presented with all kinds of improbable mélanges, employing a near-infinitude of esoteric terms (not infrequently drawn from the world of horse breeding, which can sound jarring to the contemporary ear) to describe them. I myself had to whip out my iPhone and Google "palomino" ("a pale golden or tan-colored horse with a white mane and tail, originally bred in the southwestern US"), but I'd also grown up with other vocabulary, like "high-yellow" and "mulatto," and, in my father's house if nowhere else, those now-anachronistic and tainted terms "quadroon" and "octoroon."

What bizarre words these are. But what a perfectly simple reality they labor to conceal and contain. When you get all the way down to it, what all these elaborate, nebulous descriptors really signify is nothing more complicated than that, in the United States in the not-so-distant past, if she did not willfully break from her family and try her luck at "passing" for white, Marlow, blue eyes and all, would have been disenfranchised and subjugated like all the rest of us—the wisdom, discipline, and brilliant style of American blackness would have been her birthright, as well. And so there was for a long time something that could be understood as a more or less genuinely unified black experience—not without its terrible hardships but conversely rife with profound satisfactions—that had nothing, or very close to nothing, to do with strict genetic markers. Indeed, even though the absurdity of race is always most pellucid at the margins, my daughter's case wouldn't even have been considered marginal in the former slave states where theories about hypodescent were most maniacally observed and a person with as undetectable an amount as one thirty-second "black blood" could be "legally" designated "colored." Which is only to say, despite all of the horrifically cruel implications of so-called one-drop laws, until relatively quite recently there was a space reserved for someone like Marlow fully within the idea of what used to be called the American Negro.

Today that impulse toward unquestioning inclusiveness (as a fully justifiable and admirable reaction to *exclusiveness*) is weakening—our words, however flawed, for people like my daughter—and even myself—gradually drifting out of the vernacular, banished wherever it is terms like "Negro" go to retire. The reason has less to do with black people suddenly forgetting their paradoxical origins* than with the idea of

---

* Though there is certainly some of that going on, too. "Speaking for myself, I know that racially charged historical moments, like this one, can increase the ever present torsion within my experience until it feels like something's got to give," Zadie Smith wrote in her 2017 *Harper's* essay "Getting In and Out," of the experience of seeing the white American artist Dana Schutz's painting *Open Casket*, which depicted the lynched black teenager Emmett Till, on show at the Whitney Biennial. "You start to yearn for absolute clarity: personal, genetic, political. I stood in front of the painting and thought how cathartic it would be if this picture filled me with rage. But it never got that deep into me, as either representation or appropriation." Soon after Smith published the piece, her own racial bona fides were called into question, partly because she had been skeptical of the racial absolutism of another "biracial" British woman, an artist called Hannah Black, who published a widely circulated letter demanding that the Whitney remove and even destroy *Open Casket*. "I do not find discussions on appropriation and representation to be in any way trivial," Smith

whiteness, and mixed-race non-blackness, continually growing, however reluctantly, less exclusive. With greater than a third of the American population now reporting at least one family member of a different race and with, since the year 2000, the option to select any combination of races on the census form, the very idea of black Americans as a fundamentally mongrel population is fraying at the seams.*

Perhaps, then, mine is the last American generation for which the logic—and illogic—of racial classifications could so easily contradict, or just gloss over, the physical protestations and nuances of the body and face. Which is one of the reasons it did initially take me by such surprise to find so many recessive traits flourishing in my daughter. I was being

---

stressed, before pointing out that Black's essentialist logic would set a Southern planter at ease. "Is Hannah Black black enough to write this letter?" Smith wondered. "Are my children too white to engage with black suffering? How black is black enough? Does an octoroon still count?"

Smith's essay "should have been titled 'Will My Mixed Children Be Black Enough for America?'" one black writer quipped on *Medium*. Another, Morgan Jerkins, addressed the essay at length on Twitter. "Black pain is not an intellectual exercise," she wrote. "Lived experiences often times transcend discourse. It's not always meant to be rationalized." "Do not be surprised," Jerkins warned, "if a chunk of that essay is used in discussions as to why biracial people need to take a backseat in the movement."

* According to the Pew Research Center: "Every U.S. census since the first one in 1790 has included questions about racial identity, reflecting the central role of race in American history from the era of slavery to current headlines about racial profiling and inequality. But the ways in which race is asked about and classified have changed from census to census, as the politics and science of race have fluctuated. And efforts to measure the multiracial population are still evolving.

"From 1790 to 1950, census takers determined the race of the Americans they counted, sometimes taking into account how individuals were perceived in their community or using rules based on their share of 'black blood.' Americans who were of multiracial ancestry were either counted in a single race or classified into categories that mainly consisted of gradations of black and white, such as mulattoes, who were tabulated with the non-white population. Beginning in 1960, Americans could choose their own race. Since 2000, they have had the option to identify with more than one."

forced to confront a truth I had, if not forgotten, certainly lost sight of for some time: my daughter does not, as so many well-meaning strangers and friends tend to put it, just "get those big blue eyes" from *maman*. But despite the length and narrowness of my own nose and the beige of my skin, I've always only been able to see a black man in the mirror staring back. One word I have never connected or been tempted to connect with myself is "biracial." The same goes for its updated variant, "multiracial." Growing up where and as I did, before the turn of the century, it simply would not have occurred to me to refer to myself as such.

Marlow's life, I now could grasp, wasn't going to be lived on my terms. But since newborns require only joy and care, not judgment or relentless inspection, and since there were many more pressing and practical concerns animating my household in those early, innocent months, it's no exaggeration to say that, while I was never unaware of it, it wasn't until later that I began paying close attention again to the way my daughter *looked*.

When she was a rosy-cheeked, towheaded four months old, I took her on our first father-daughter excursion. It was a big deal for me. Her mother had just returned to work and was no longer breastfeeding, and I had never assumed so much responsibility before. Equipped with a fluffy bag of the requisite baby paraphernalia, we set off from our apartment to the Gare Saint-Lazare, where we boarded a regional train to its terminus in Deauville, a picturesque nineteenth century resort town on the Atlantic coast in Normandy. During the two-hour ride, the two of us dozed and ate, and I gazed at my daughter in paternal awe. I was still learning her face, locating in its singularity what seemed like dimples from *maman*, a pair of wide, laughing eyes perhaps from me, and a newfound grimace, awkwardly beguiling, that was hers alone.

Steve came to meet our train. Marlow and I would spend a few days with him and his son Jo-Jo in the country, to give our wives some respite and to drink bottles of his parents' Burgundy by the fire once the children were in bed. A perfect French idyll, as far as I'm concerned. Steve and his family are chocolatiers. We bundled into his car and, along the way, stopped in the town center to see their new shop. He also wanted to introduce his niece to his siblings who were supervising the opening of the store. I lifted my daughter in my arms and carried her inside. Filled with that incommunicable pride that comes with the simple feat of parenthood, I passed the baby around and helped myself to some confections.

By then I'd become aware that Marlow's hardly-mixed looks could strike some people as anticlimactic or, worse, please them excessively, both reactions that leave me ill at ease. Family and close friends like Steve, one of the gentlest people I know, on some level intuit this. Which is why it caught me like an errant elbow when his sister, certainly not intending harm and simply voicing what many others must have thought, picked up Marlow and exclaimed, "Wow, but were you even in the room, or did Valentine simply reproduce herself?" I laughed, and Steve made a diplomatic remark about the similarity of our personalities, but when we climbed back in the car I studied Marlow's face for traces of myself—which I did find there—and wondered why these remained so inscrutable to everyone else.

A quarter hour down the road from where we were headed is Valentine's grandmother's home, where two years prior we'd been married. Before the ceremony, I remember strolling across the property with my father, just the two of us; he was handsome and formal in his suit. We stopped beneath an apple tree overlooking the carp ponds and neighboring cow pastures and little Norman outbuildings all over the lawn, with their dark columns and white plaster walls, little gingerbread houses that epitomize all kinds of things that we are not. My father turned to me with an expression that was tender and, I think, also somewhat grave, and told me, *Son, don't lose yourself.* He wasn't scolding me, and he wasn't stern—he seemed almost to be imploring me or perhaps not even addressing me at all but speaking through me to some younger him. I'm not sure. We were interrupted shortly after, and I had to step away. We never resumed that conversation, but his words still come back to me and only grow louder with each passing year.

Several years earlier, it would not have occurred to him to say something like that to me. My situation looked very different from the outside now, though from the inside it is difficult to locate the decisive moment at which your life becomes what it will be—to sift from the mound of experiences that single grain—or even that fistful—of sand that shattered the back of one identity to allow the possibility of the next. I couldn't say when it happened to me, but one day I realized that I am frequently in rooms where not a single other soul is black. At times, in a twist that I am sure is unusual for an African-American, race recedes from my lived experience and becomes something wholly cerebral, abstract. In going about getting my daily bread, in making chitchat with the baker or rattling off the few Italian phrases I've been able to pick up over the years with the amiable grocer from Turin, I can forget about my racial categorization entirely, a sense of existential levity I don't believe my father has ever known. In any event, it comes and goes. Some inner mechanism tends to yank me back, and I am aware again that the room is white. And I realize, too, that I have grown comfortable in these rooms, though I don't feel myself to be white, not at all. Then I look at my daughter and wonder: In all of these white rooms that she is being brought up in, what will she learn to think of herself? Will she develop my ancestral GPS, or will that signal fade—would it even be right for me to transmit my habits of orientation, some of which are riddled with guilt and steeped in illusion, to her untroubled head?

OVER THE COURSE of that stay in Normandy chez Steve, I took dozens, perhaps even hundreds of photos of Marlow with my phone—as she dozed on my bed or stared at the horses grazing the lawn, as we drove to the beach, not far at all from where her great-grandfather (on my mother's side), who never fully acclimated himself to the idea of his black progeny, would have arrived as an Army sergeant in '44, on his way to liberating concentration camps in Germany. (That foreign evil, of course, was one that he could grasp and correctly despise even as he remained oblivious to and even complicit in other, subtler evils at home.) In the pictures I took of my daughter, I found myself applying filters that made her skin tone tanner. I erased shots that looked too washed out, overexposed. Out of many, I found one in which she appeared virtually ecru, and this I forwarded to friends. If I felt strange conspiring to manage my daughter's looks, I was also pleased and even relieved to have visual testimony that she was, however faintly, "black" in the most extraordinarily elastic sense of the term. And this photograph, along with a battered but still-obedient adherence to the one-drop rule and the conviction that Steve's French family, like so many non-Americans, simply don't know the greater truth, bought me several more months of unexamined life.

There's another image of my daughter that I keep at my apartment and often return to as I write. In this one, she's twenty months and seated on a large green couch in the house my brother has rented for my parents' fortieth wedding anniversary. Next to her is my brother's daughter, Mila, a gorgeously mixed half-Russian ten-month-old with her father's olive skin and bushy eyebrows and her mother's thick blond locks and azure eyes. In the picture, the two cousins are staring at each other, smiling. To the right of Mila, half obscured by the teddy bear she's hugging, sits the life-sized ebony baby doll my mother has given to Marlow. It is tucked in the corner, either an afterthought or a reminder, its wide, brown, unblinking eyes peering over the bear and straight into my lens. The image conveys to me a wry question: *Which of these is a real black baby, and which is artificial?* And yet if I linger on the image, stare a little longer, another memory surfaces: the way we filled the house with Bobby "Blue" Bland and Syl Johnson, John Coltrane and

Nina Simone, the way these sounds stir Marlow from the couch and induce her to bop rapturously to the beat. These are also her sounds if she wants them. When she bops a little too close to the stairs leading down to the basement, I witness my seventy-eight-year-old father shed years from his age and pounds from his arthritic frame to explode from the dinner table, like a sprinter out of the block, faster than Valentine can move from the kitchen, indeed faster than I find myself moving, and grab his granddaughter before she has the chance to fall. He pulls her to him and she laughs. They have the same smile.

Later that evening, Pappy will tell me again, as he told me while holding Marlow in Paris, that he could see no incongruity between the appearances of these little girls and what anyone else might describe as being "black." Some of his classmates in his segregated Texas schools looked just like these girls. "It has always been this way," he insists. "The notion of the 'other' is false." False or not, though, Marlow's birth and presence in my life did upend my sense of myself and give me a closer glimpse of the fluidity of racial borders than most people who did not grow up on the black side of town in the Jim Crow South have ever had to consider, if only because social custom tends to keep the vast majority of us so far away from the edges. That distance allows us to resort to crude color metaphors without the risk of cognitive dissonance that necessarily attaches to a statement like, *My father is black but my daughter is white*. What does a black face even look like? I used to try—and, if I'm honest, sometimes still catch myself trying—to answer that question. "But any fool can see that the white people are not really white, and that black people are not black," the writer Albert Murray was fond of pointing out. It's an observation so basic and obviously true that it's almost impossible to take seriously, like insisting that the sun does not, in fact, rise or set. But what does it say about us that the most common means we have to describe ourselves rely on categories that do not and cannot manifest on human flesh?

John Locke observed that categories "are made by the mind and not by nature"; how indeed can you learn to look at yourself in the mirror and actually *see* what's there without the background noise of prejudice and myth? I can think of very few things that I have tried to do that have been harder. I don't think I'm alone at this, either. After all these generations and centuries of practice, we still don't know how to see and talk about ourselves or each other. We are at the same time obsessed with "race" and wholly confounded by it. As our memories of the first black presidency congeal, I must, like you, perform some slight rhetorical legerdemain every time I define the Obama administration as such. It is very difficult to recall that it was the first openly part-African-descended presidency. It's not only that such a formulation would be awfully anticlimactic; it's also that we viscerally believe in our boxes and, recent census efforts notwithstanding, don't *really* know or want to know how to let a person stand comfortably in two—or more—at the same time.* This is why in America, and in no other country

---

* A 2010 *New York Times* article headlined "Asked to Declare His Race, Obama Checks 'Black'" noted, "The president, who was born in Hawaii and raised there and in Indonesia, had more than a dozen options in responding to Question 9, about race. He chose 'Black, African Am., or Negro.'" But he could have "checked white,

I am aware of, we produce "black" presidents like Barack Hussein Obama, "black" activists like the blue-eyed star of *Grey's Anatomy* Jesse Williams and the ostracized quarterback Colin Kaepernick, and "black" and virtually white-skinned NAACP leaders like Benjamin Jealous and Walter White decades before him. The example of White resonates with me in particular: pale-skinned, blue-eyed, and blond-haired, he could be the male version of Marlow. "Many Negroes are judged as whites," he wrote in his 1948 autobiography *A Man Called White*. "Every year approximately twelve-thousand white-skinned Negroes disappear—people whose absence cannot be explained by death or emigration." It has *always* been this way, I can hear my father say.

Still, we rush into our boxes, sealing the sides around us. That we now recognize there are some people who really should occupy two at a time paradoxically only reinforces the false certainty that the rest of us should not. The idea that the boxes we sort ourselves into are not and have never been real is another question altogether, one we sometimes pay rote lip service to but haven't come to terms with anywhere near the level of conviction. We are a nation content to live in a state of collective bad faith, like Sartre's coquette on the bench, willingly misinterpreting the evidence in hand, refusing to draw the implied conclusions.

"The worst thing one can do with words is to surren-

---

checked both black and white, or checked the last category on the form, 'some other race.'" Interestingly, though a majority of Americans polled by the Pew Research Center in 2014 described Obama as "mixed-race" and not as "black," it's unclear whether those same respondents would view the former category as part of the latter or as distinct.

der to them." George Orwell said that. "Black," "white," "mixed," "person of color" . . . all of us live under the weight of these labels—even those of us whose existence can't help but defy them. In color theory, there is no such thing as white—it exists solely in our perception of the world, not as a color per se but as the absence of such. In real life, too, the lived experience of "whiteness" is often construed as the absence of racial identity. It is the neutral starting point from which all else constitutes a deviation. *A drop of black blood makes a person black because they are disqualified from being white.* Blackness, on the other hand, is color at its most concentrated. Yet it, too, is meaningless outside the presence of white. "The blackness of typescript doesn't mean that the letters are actually black," notes the Japanese graphic designer Kenya Hara. "They merely appear black in contrast to a white sheet of paper."

I do not appear black to my own daughter because she has not yet learned how to draw the necessary contrasts. As I write, she is four, and I have told her I am what we call black, but this has not convinced her. "You are beige," she responds. She is not color-blind. She recognizes that her Papi de Paris, her French granddad, is what we call white—though when he has had some wine, she astutely points out that he is actually *rose* or pink. And she grasps that her Papi de New York, or American granddad, is "brown," as she naïvely or shrewdly puts it. These are obvious facts of being she accepts with equal indifference. In addition to that, she knows and accepts that her mother is called white, and when she looks in the mirror at her big blue eyes and mass of blond curls, I can only conclude that she believes that she is the same, no matter how many *If I Had a Dinosaur* books I read to her with protagonists who are black. These are some of the reasons that, in the fall of 2016, I finally went ahead, after years of equivocating, and ordered a kit to test my DNA. To speak about a thing clearly you must first be able to name it. To speak about yourself, you must first be able to assemble a sense of origin. For descendants of slaves, this has proved one of the most precious losses of self-knowledge we've endured. The black experience in the South is tantamount to the biblical flood; we've stumbled off the ark without an inkling of what things were like before it. Without genetic testing, as flawed and incomplete as it may be, we wouldn't even be able to say with confidence from which country— let alone linguistic community or tribe—we were uprooted. In this land, we've become homogenized into something totally new. But whites in the United States also have a way of dissolving into each other, shrugging off the sharp lines of ethnic specificity. My mother's mother grew up speaking German to her immigrant parents in Baltimore. But as so often happens, the Old World was the last thing on anybody's mind by the time her daughter was bronzing her shoulders on the beaches of Southern California.

For my part, I have lived most of my life in America, nine significant years in Western Europe, mostly France, some months in Argentina, and have traveled often and extensively as far east as Moscow and Saint Petersburg. Each of these places has rubbed off on me in ways both subtle and explicit, to the point that the New Jersey of my youth can feel like the most foreign territory. But I have never set foot in Africa below Morocco, have never felt the warmth of that particular sun on my body. I write this now in freezing Berlin, a tab on my laptop displaying a pastel pie chart of my ancestral-geographical makeup. I scrutinize the color-coded slices for meaning. That fuchsia "Sub-Saharan" segment is markedly less than half—39.9 percent of the pie—though that is where my received social identity, as well as (what the website identifies as) my most recent non-American ancestor, came from, sometime between 1830 and 1890. The marine-blue "European" section, on the other hand—which I always understood existed but nonetheless thought of as existing somehow outside of *me*—comprises some 58.7 percent of the circle, almost all of it northern. This lopsided ratio surprised me, though it should not have. As far back as 1970, some 24 percent of white Americans (a figure nearly twice the black population at the time) had some African ancestry—often without knowing it, often the result of some wily predecessor successfully having slipped the yoke. But that was not the case in my mother's family. My aunt came back 99.9 percent European. Presuming she and my mother share all ancestors, that would put my father at just under 80 percent African—right on average, as it happens, for the mixed, Afro-European population of Americans we refer to as "black."

The results also let me know I do not have the Alzheimer's trait, and I am relieved as my mind turns to the kind face of my maternal grandmother, ravaged by dementia to the point that she smiled shyly, saying ,"Hi, I'm Esther," the last time I saw her over a seafood dinner in San Diego. She had forgotten her own daughter's name but not that German she grew up speaking in her parents' house. This aspect of her identity, my mother marvels, she held on to completely, tenaciously even. Were I to endure a similar fate, I wonder what would be the essence I would revert to,

I close the tab. A pie chart will not tell me who or what I am. My daughter's identity reflects back at me and changes me not just down the line but today, in the present. I would be another person if she were Japanese. And I would be another person still if she were Puerto Rican. I can see the Russianness of my niece impacting my brother in real time even as I marvel at how rapidly my sister-in-law is Americanizing. Is this not why groups like the aristocracy fought so hard to maintain the boundaries of lineage? They knew that human beings are malleable and fleeting things. I want to suggest that one becomes, in part, one's children and grandchildren every bit as much as one carries within herself one's parents and grandparents.* I want to say that I will no longer enter into the all-American skin game that demands you select a box and define yourself by it. And it *is a game*, not in the sense of entertainment but in the sense of game theory—a veritable prisoner's dilemma in which we are all trapped though highly unlikely to escape, since self-interest mixed with ignorance of each other's intentions practically ensures we make the wrong decision.

I have resolved to take a gamble and walk away, the incomprehensible round of the genetic pie chart still glowing on the backs of my eyelids when I shut them. I am well aware that our situation is not yet—and may not ever be—

---

* "A Jew today," as one particularly forbidding saying goes, "is anyone who has Jewish grandchildren."

a common one, and that I have experienced a specific set of breaks and good fortune outside of my own control that have contributed powerfully to my own sense of autonomy in the world. I was born into a loving, two-parent home, encouraged and instructed from a very young age to read and study by an unusually erudite father, crucially provided throughout my adolescence with the time to do it, and, perhaps just as decisively in retrospect, exposed to what is understood as "whiteness" through my mother and some of her family in non-antagonistic, positively nurturing ways that left me fundamentally at ease with and unsuspicious of the broader American culture.

"For most African-Americans, white people exist either as a direct or an indirect force for bad in their lives," Ta-Nehisi Coates observed in his 2016 essay on Barack Obama, "My President Was Black." "Biraciality is no shield against this," he cautioned, "often it just intensifies the problem." Obama's rare advantage, then, in Coates's view, had more than a little to do with the fact that "the first white people he ever knew, the ones who raised him, were decent in a way that very few black people of that era experienced." This was my reality, too.

And though there has been massive societal change since Obama's youth in the 1960s, or even my own in the 1980s, I am equally aware that such a description continues to resonate, and that most so-called "black" people do not feel themselves at liberty to simply turn off or ignore their allotted racial designation, whether they would like to or not. But that doesn't mean that they *shouldn't*. Nor does it mean that people who are considered to be white and who are so often encouraged to move through social life *un-raced* shouldn't become more aware of the ways in which their racial identity has been made, in order that they, too, might learn to consciously reject it. In fact, it is crucial that they do. Whether it results from vicious bigotry or well-meaning anti-racism is of secondary concern: essentialism—what James Baldwin described as the "insistence that it is [one's] categorization alone which is real and which cannot be transcended"—is always an evasion of life; the beautiful truth, in all its terrifying complexity, is that we all contain multitudes. Purity is always a lie, though it is a lie that is certainly most ostentatious when the "mixing" is freshest.

What I hope to explore here, through my own family's multigenerational transformation from what is called "black" to what is assumed to be "white"—which is to say, through my own confrontation with the fiction of race—are ways of seeing and relating to each other that operate somewhere between the poles of tribal identitarianism and Panglossian utopianism. People will always look different from each other in ways we can't control. What we can control is what we allow ourselves to make of those differences.

The idea of racial categorization is an old one, but it is not an ancient one. We know that the Roman playwright Terence observed, "I am human, therefore nothing human is alien to me." And we know that Imperial Rome was a dizzyingly cosmopolitan milieu, men and women speaking all manner of tongues, worshipping all manner of gods, displaying all manner of skin tones moving through it. And yet it's worth lingering a moment longer on the fact that Terence did *not* proclaim, as he might have, "I am Roman, therefore nothing *Roman* is alien to me." It has become a commonplace to acknowledge the following point, but it bears repeating anyway: the idea of distinct human races, as we understand it today, only stretches back to Enlightenment Europe, which is to say to the eighteenth century. I have stayed in inns in Germany and eaten at taverns in Spain that have been continuously operating longer than this calamitous thought.

With the publication of *Systema Naturae*, in 1735, Carl Linnaeus, the Swedish naturalist and "father of modern taxonomy," fatefully split mankind into four color-coded strands, *Europaeus albus*, *Americanus rubescens*, *Asiaticus fuscus*, *Africanus niger*; later, the German naturalist, "father of anthropology," and coiner of that confused and confusing term "Caucasian," * Johann Friedrich Blumenbach, would have us be five, the aforementioned "Caucasian" (white), "Mongolian" (yellow), "Malayan" (brown), "Ethiopian" (black), and "American" (red), though to his credit he deemphasized hierarchical thinking. The divisions have always been somewhat arbitrary and imprecise, and have fluctuated many times since. What these scientists were attempting, however inadequately, was simply to describe the real physical differences that they observed in the world around them. In Sweden and Germany, such pursuits were fundamentally abstract. The social

---

* Nell Irvin Painter, in *The History of White People*, makes the fascinating point that the term derives from an ideal of white physical beauty popularized through odalisque paintings depicting fair-skinned slave women from the Caucuses held in Turkish harems. In other words, the language of white supremacy is rooted, incongruously, in depictions of white servitude and literal inferiority.

and political significance of race and what we've come to understand as white supremacy—how it came to be lived on the ground—was something only fully being realized in the collision, en masse, of these different-looking peoples in the New World through conquest and slavery. (This is also why, to this day, many Africans who remained in Africa have never thought of themselves as "black.")

It was in the New World that race—and more important, racism—"emerged from a fundamental imbalance in power among social groups," as the historian Jacqueline Jones observes in *A Dreadful Deceit.* "On slave ships transporting men, women, and children from their homelands to the New World, European captors became white and their African captives became black. Over time these two adjectives each took on multiple meanings, with white signifying 'someone free and descended from free forebears,' and black signifying 'someone enslaved or descended from slaves.'" The social and political, as opposed to scientific, significance of the binary is obvious in the maddeningly whimsical nature of one colonial law, which first declared the legal—and therefore racial—status of mixed-race children to be transmitted via the father, only to be subsequently reversed to the mother.* Before tradition took hold, these were distinctions set in wet cement and not in stone.

Yet the color hierarchy that emerged from this lopsided,

---

* This was so that white male slave owners could continue to sleep with their black slaves without fear of producing illegitimate "mixed-race" children in possession of legal claims to inheritance. Thus it turned a potential liability into a winning situation: enslaved "black" offspring became a source of *more* wealth instead of a drain on it.

centuries-long encounter—even in the absence of slavery and subsequent legalized oppression—has proven extraordinarily resilient and highly transferable, as capable of global scale as sugar and cotton production, though it has never found a more rigid logic than in the United States of America. I was reminded of this fact one sunny autumn day in Berlin, where I lived far out on the city's western edge. Across the placid Lake Wannsee stood a stately Italianate summer villa that once belonged to a Jewish industrialist before it was stolen by the Nazis, whose leadership infamously gathered there, over a ninety-minute lunch, to settle upon their final solution. The House of the Wannsee Conference now functions as a museum, a sobering testament to the boundless monstrosity that can arise from the desire to sort and bind people into racial categories. The walls inside are plastered with images that make the blood at turns boil then freeze, grainy photographs of pogroms and massacres and jaunty propaganda, which the far-right Alternative für Deutschland Party has begun to recycle today, urging the people to create "full-blooded" German babies for the greater good.

I visited the house with my college best friend, Marlow's godfather, Josh, himself a descendant of Eastern European Jews. We drifted through the rooms at different speeds, and soon I found myself facing a large illustrated display detailing the Nuremberg Laws, which were of course concerned first and foremost with measuring Jewish descent, but they also—and even more stringently—sought to codify who would count as black. The Nazis were famously inspired by the practices of Southern whites, and it shows. (The first anti-miscegenation statute in the United States, which affected marriage, dates all the way back to 1661 in Maryland. It didn't prohibit marriage between whites and blacks, but it did enslave white women who married black men.)

I studied those mixture tables, the ominous circles marked *Deutschblütiger*, *Mischling*, and *Jude* that were shaded with pseudo-precision to varying degrees. I lingered over their insanely meticulous rationale. Then one excerpt in particular caught my eye: "Pursuant to article 6 of the first supplementary decree of the Law for the Protection of German Blood, marriage should be prohibited if it is likely to result in offspring that would taint the purity of German blood. This decree prohibits marriage between persons of German blood and those of foreign blood, even if they are not carriers of Jewish blood. . . . Negro blood is so strong that its influence is frequently still clearly visible among members of the 7th or 8th generation. In cases where the intended spouse carries Negro blood a particularly thorough examination will therefore be required, the results of which will determine whether the marriage is permissible."

It was wildly unnerving, even all these decades removed, suddenly to feel that Nazi gaze, however brief and distracted it may have been, channeling the hatred of the Southern slaver and turning itself on *me*. Because of the codifications the Third Reich so militantly tried to impose, since the Second World War, in academia and the mainstream media and respectable discourse throughout the world more generally, such racially essentialist ways of speaking about identity have been overwhelmingly discredited, which is, of course, all to the good. Now we prefer to rely on euphemistic terms such as "culture," "ethnicity," "nationality," "ancestry," and, if we're being more current, "genetic pools," to make sense of inevitable human variety. And yet beneath this enlightened veneer of politesse and scientific rigor, when we resort to received habits of speech, uncritically describing ourselves and others with abstractions like "black" and "white" and "half-black," or when we discuss—approvingly or not—the presence in our backgrounds of "Jewish" or "Native American" *blood*, is the underlying logic really all that evolved?* Or is it possible that there has been left over some ideological residue—from the Nazis, from the Southern planters before them, or, going further back still, from the Spanish, who created the first *limpieza de sangre* laws to separate "old Christians" from those who carried Muslim and Jewish taint?

My goal here is to refute, however difficult that may prove to be, such persistent and flattening thinking that has led to so much human suffering, precluded and squandered so much human potential. To do so, whiteness—the disastrous illusion undergirding all aspects of race—will have to be overcome. Yet I am also aware that the proud and resilient identities that have formed in reaction to its construction may be, in some ways, even harder to convert. Recently, during a question-and-answer period after a talk

---

* And for a current example of lingering and problematic conceptions of the potency of "blood," take the case of Senator Elizabeth Warren. Beginning from a well-meaning, anti-racist stance, she ended up reinforcing the basic race-essentialist tenets on display in the Nuremberg Laws—and swiftly drew rebuke from members of the Cherokee nation and others—in attempting to establish, through gene testing, a meaningful Native American ancestry.

I gave on the same subject at a liberal arts college in upstate New York, a young dark-skinned sophomore from Queens, child of Jamaican immigrants, rose to his feet and told me in no uncertain terms that he thought I was woefully naïve and frankly out of touch to imagine a social reality beyond the dictates of race. He was not ambiguous-looking and could not conceive of a world in which he was not "black, period"—despite the fact that his West Indian ethnicity and personal trajectory as a child of striving immigrants would necessarily and rather meaningfully differentiate him from the descendants of Southern slaves, many of whose lines have been in America longer than almost any other group. The subject was closed, he said, primarily because "black" is how the "whites" he interacted with in this rural town invariably saw him. "It's who I am," he said as he equated an allegiance to a color-coded racial category with loyalty to the working-class New York City community he came from, which he juxtaposed with the isolating college campus on which he now found himself. Because race—in our imaginations most of all, but that is crucial—is so often *classed*, I empathized with his position immediately. I had also experienced some of these same misgivings when I was his age and acclimating to life in a wealthy university town that was light-years away from the place where I'd been raised. Very often a class transition, without any further complicating factors needed, can feel just like a racial one. I understood exactly why this student so adamantly—and courageously, given the dynamics of the room—made his case to me. But it is a case based on at least two presumptions that deserve a great deal more skepticism all the same. The first is that one's inner sense of self ought to derive from and even be held hostage by the ignorance or mistaken thinking of those with whom one is fated to be neighbors. I myself would be an Arab today were I to allow the perceptive habits and assumptions of French society to identify me.* The second is that a flawed paradigm cannot be reimagined and shifted in the future simply because we are dealing with its practical consequences as they exist today.

I would not deny that "colorism"—which is typically defined as "prejudice or discrimination against individuals with a dark skin tone, typically among people of the same ethnic or racial group," but for most intents and purposes simply means that people with lighter skin tend to have it easier—is real and likely informs every aspect of my own thinking. It informs it, and has perhaps made my own effort that much less daring, but it does not define it. I am not renouncing my *blackness* and going on about my day; I am rejecting the legitimacy of the entire racial construct in which blackness functions as one orienting pole. The student that I spoke with can and should reject race, too, I submit, because it is a mistake for any of us to reify something that is as demonstrably harmful as it is fictitious. Visibly and recently "mixed" people may have the most obvious rhetorical means of doing this, but I would also encourage ostensibly "white" and "Asian"† people to make the same linguistic

---

* The caveat here, of course, is that once I open my mouth the assumption becomes implausible.

† Race is most fully expressed along a conceptual "black-white" binary, but purportedly explanatory terms like "Asian," "person of color," or even "Latino" also collapse

maneuver. I am not so ingenuous as to think everyone can *want* to reconceive themselves, but I do believe the more that people of good will—white, black, and everything in between—try, the more the rigidity of our collective faith in race will necessarily soften.

I think of this student and I am reminded of another dark-skinned man I have come to know and admire, Kmele Foster, a New York–based entrepreneur and public thinker who, for a variety of rigorous and principled reasons, refuses to identity himself as black. Mixed-race people, light-skinned blacks, and others who do not suffer the full weight of skin bias certainly can form an avant-garde when it comes to rejecting race. But Foster, whose wife and child are also unambiguously brown-skinned, shows by example that an intellectual stance impervious to other people's expectations is possible for all of us. Of course, the most common response to his position is dismissive: "Yeah, okay, that's all well and good, but wait until you have a run-in with the police, and then you'll see just how black you are." I take seriously the raw pain and historical experience that is behind such an objection, and I do not claim that the criminal justice system is without tremendous bias (most crushingly against the poor). But this is not an argument; it's a threat, an appeal to an event that has not yet happened. As such, it is impossible to disprove a counterfactual claim. Yet even if Kmele were to be racially profiled and abused tomorrow,

---

under scrutiny. An "extreme example of inconsistency in the classification by race over time," according to a Census Bureau working paper, "is that a person counted as an Asian Indian since 1980 could have been classified three other ways in earlier censuses: Hindu in 1920–1940, 'other race' in 1950–1960 and white in 1970."

horrific as that would be, it still would not be reason for him to revise his fundamental understanding of himself in order to better conform to the damaging prejudices of the racist who targeted him. It would make no more sense for him to do this than it would for me, given the numerous instances I have been profiled, detained, and questioned in airports, to accept and internalize the misperception that I am from the Middle East.*

The truth is that ideas matter. Our language, formal and informal alike, shapes our reality. The terminology we use and accept to be used matters. The images we make and allow to be made of ourselves matter, as do the narratives we recite in order to tell ourselves, and each other, who we are, where we come from, and where we think we are going. If we really want to repair what is wrong in our society, it is going to require not just new policies or even new behaviors, but nothing less heroic than new ideas.

"While social repair does not happen at scale," as the columnist David Brooks has argued, "it happens in rooms one by one and those things build up and slowly change norms and norms do scale." My wish, in the most fundamental sense, is to show how the idea of race has unraveled in my own life so that it might spark some of that much-needed repair, one-on-one, in whatever room you may happen to find yourself. Perhaps you may then bring that spark with you into the next room, and so on. I am not ashamed to repeat now what I told that college student when he berated

---

* This is *not* to say that were I in fact from the Middle East such instances of baseless discrimination then would be justified.

me. I think he was right in at least one very important regard: A certain degree of naïveté is what is needed *most* if we are ever to solve the tragedy of racism in the absence of human races. We already know where self-certain oversophistication inevitably leads us.

PART ONE

||

**THE VIEW FROM
NEAR AND FAR**

'D LEFT THE CAFETERIA, WHERE MY BROTHER CLARENCE was racing the wooden kit car he'd taught himself how to carpenter with the older Boy Scouts, and made my way down the long corridor to the restroom. The building was virtually empty on a Saturday and charged with that faint lawlessness of school not in session. When I'd finished, I fixed myself in the mirror and, on the way out, ran and leaped to swing from the high bar joining the metal stalls to the tiled wall. In the third grade, this was hard to do, a feat of superior athleticism that I savored even in the absence of a witness. I had the same bounce in my legs that linked me with my favorite athletes. I wore my hair like them, too, shaved low on the sides and back and slightly higher on top with a laser-sharp part engraved on the left. As my feet thrust forward, the door shot open and Evan stepped in. An eighth-grader, the eldest of three freckled, blond, almost farcically preppy brothers—still an Irish Catholic but WASPier than the sons of Italians, Poles, and Ukrainians who formed the backbone of the student body at our parochial school—he watched me dismount. In his costume of boat shoes and Dockers, Evan was far from an intimidating sight, but he was bigger than me, and he smiled at me strangely. I made to pass him on the way out, but he blocked me, his smile turning menacing. "What?" I managed, confused. We'd been in school together for years without ever having exchanged a word. "Monkey," he whispered, still smiling, and my whole body froze: I was being insulted—in an ugly way, I could sense from his expression more than from what was said—but I couldn't fully grasp why. I'd been swinging like a monkey, it was true, but this was something else. I tried again to step around him, at a loss for words; he blocked my way again, looming over me, still with that smirk. "You little fucking *monkey*," he repeated with deliberate calm, and to my astonishment I realized that, although I could not understand why, there was, however vague and out of place, suddenly the possibility of violence. Out of nothing more than instinct, I shoved past him with all the determination an eight-year-old can gather.

This time he let me go, and I could hear his laughter behind me as I made my way back to the cafeteria, my heart pumping staccato, my face singed with the heat of self-awareness, my inexperienced mind fumbling for the meaning behind what had just transpired. I also knew enough to know that I could not tell my father what had happened. I could see his reaction—see him shoot from his leather desk chair where he spent the majority of weekends as well as weekdays bent over a book, underlining, learning, focusing. "Let's go," he'd say in a clipped tone, with that distant look in his eyes, like he was looking at something else, not at me, and by that time he would already be at the hall closet throwing his dark gray overcoat over his broad shoulders, keys jangling in his strong hand. As he'd push through the door, me trailing behind, I could be certain that his chin would already be slightly lowered, as if in anticipation of the blow he would deflect and then counter with everything he had—with even more, perhaps, than the situation demanded. If I were to have told him what that white boy had said to me in the restroom, Pappy would have descended into an indescribable fury the memory of which can tense me up to this day. He would have lost a week of work and concentration—that was as certain as two and two is four. But I also knew that he would be shot through with pain, unable to sleep, up at his desk in the dark, transported to his past, agonizing over this awful proof of what he'd always suspected: that no matter how strong *he* was, he was not strong enough to shield—not fully—his sons from the psychological warfare of American racism that whispers obscenities at little boys when they find themselves alone. It was far too expensive a cost to bear. On that day and on other days after that, I resolved myself to be strong enough to shield *him* from knowing these truths.

My father's fury over the past, over the mind-boggling injustice of lesser men and even their children thinking they had something over him because of nothing greater than the tint of skin and weft of hair, was something I did not fully share. Rather, it was something I learned very early to empathize with in my deepest core—the ultimately incommunicable ache of someone I loved as I loved myself, knowable but not my own—and to anticipate as best I could. I failed to do this one gorgeous fall afternoon when Pappy made the trip himself to pick me up from school. It was special and it was different riding alongside my father. The radio remained off; there would be no Hot 97, as there might be with my mother, to deformalize the encounter and put it more on my terms. There would be instead adult-like questions followed by the expectation of well-thought-out replies.

"How was your day, son?"

Pappy seemed in a good mood. It was hot outside. He'd showered and powdered his neck—the smell of talc and the pomade he sometimes used to brush his hair sweetening the old car leather into the most impressive musk. The car was idling but we hadn't pulled out. Classmates whose parents hadn't arrived lingered in the sidewalk's shade. Somehow we began to speak about sports, which ones I was good at and which might intrigue me. Basketball was my great love, but in those days baseball mattered, too. "And boxing?" Pappy asked. "It's about time you learn to box. You want to be able to box, don't you?"

I sensed a level of approval in the way he was regarding me. I was old enough now to be let in on this masculine secret. Intellectual development was paramount to my father, of course, but he was hardly a geek. He was a man who happened to be of a certain Southern culture and a certain age, and his talents and tastes had been molded accordingly. That I was not only academically inclined but physically promising pleased him, and both aspects of the self were to be cultivated, that was obviously true.

The sun shone warmly on me through the windshield, relaxing my mind, which wandered ahead into my room to lose my uniform and rush outside to play. I was already racing to the basketball courts and I missed the gravity of my father's query, mistook him in that moment for a different, more casual kind of interlocutor. "Oh, I don't know, Babe,"* I said distractedly. "I don't really care that much about boxing."

"You don't *care* about boxing?" he repeated. "Who told you that?"

"No one told me that. What do you mean?"

Pappy's face tightened. I remember: the ignition churning; that old Benz three-point-turning; Pappy gesturing at my very white classmates idling. "Who *told* you not to like boxing?"

"But no one did!" I didn't even understand the question. "Goddammit!"

I had not yet spent significant time with the other black boys I would come to know and acculturate myself to, the boys from the redlined peripheries of my small town who were a lot like the boys from the larger, all-black neighborhoods beyond it, boys who looked older than me even when they were younger, who threw their hands at each other habitually—and skillfully—both in earnestness and in jest. I was still a few years away from familiarity with any of that, and boxing was something that I had only ever seen my father do. I remember the enormous, generations-old frustration in his exclamation in the car. And a possessive kind of fear. I don't remember whatever I could have said to him in return, whatever I must have stammered to save myself and calm him down. I do remember his astonishing wounded rage that seemed to have very little, in fact, to do with *me*—or at least with who I thought myself to be—when

---

* We call my father "Babe" when directly addressing him, kind of like the *tu* to the formal *vous* of "Pappy." It's because, as a small child, my brother constantly heard his mother call her husband "baby," and simply thought this was his name. Likewise, I could imagine another scenario in which we all came to call him "Honey."

he shouted, for the first and only time in my life, "I'll be *damned* if they make you white!" And I remember the most excruciating silence for the duration of the ride back home, as my brain fumbled around the notion that you could be made into something you knew you could not be.

Not long after that, when the mood had passed—and that was the other thing, these eruptions of the deepest racial hurt and fear came like flash floods in July, as fleeting as they were unexpected—I approached my father to tell him I wanted to learn. His father had not been a part of his life, and his mother had passed when I was an infant. We did not know his extended family from Texas. From time to time, once a year or less frequently, the phone would ring and Pappy's voice would grow folksier, maybe even slower, and he would chat with some other relation for an hour, sometimes more. I tried to conjure the faces of these phantom men and women who—incredibly, to me—knew who my father was, knew from what world he had come, but imagine as I would, I had no idea what lives they might lead. "Oh, that's so-and-so from Detroit," my mother might say, as if that could clarify matters for me. When Pappy hung up, whatever link had been temporarily forged with the past immediately receded from our home, and it was obvious the subject was closed. Sometimes, when I asked him how he learned to fight so well, he would get a gentle, wistful look in the eye and say that his uncles in Longview had shown him how—one of the few memories of home I'm aware of that could provoke a wholly uncomplicated smile.

I should have better understood how fundamental boxing must have been to my father's sense of himself as a man in the world, as fundamental as books. After all, the evidence, like those books, was all around me. Our basement could have been decorated by Cus D'Amato if he had a literary bent. We had a treadmill, stationary bikes, and resistance machines, in addition to medicine balls, benches, and weights. There was a professional-grade heavy bag and a speed bag in the garage, as well as full sets of headgear and scarlet-red Everlast gloves. Only looking back on it now do I realize that my father must have anticipated that he would train us. There would be intermittent lessons throughout my childhood and adolescence, moments of instruction snatched in the hallway or kitchen in which he patiently demonstrated to me where to place my feet, how to hunch my shoulders—chin down, protect the neck—and how to parry a blow. "Bend your knees and keep your feet planted like this so you can respond." Pappy was unhittable, at least for me, whip-fast with the hands, torso, and head well into his sixties. My hands are quick, too. But where I am lanky, he is compact. His jaw is made firmer than mine. It was beautiful to witness what he could do. Is there anything more wonderful than watching your father soar? Perhaps, I imagine now, it is equaled only in the pleasure of transmitting—really *imparting*—something of yourself to your son.

One evening thrusts beyond the fog of childhood memory like a rocky peak glimpsed from an airplane window. Pappy takes the scrawny little boy who must have been me down into the basement, puts the gloves on his fists, and then gloves his own hands. It is a hard space, with hard tiled floors cracking to expose the concrete underneath—the most undomesticated part of the house by far. Instead of the wood upstairs, there are hard metal shelves of thousands of surplus books lining the walls, and the exercise equipment is arranged between them. There are hard black disks of iron weights and chrome bars, and the air is cool and damp on the hottest day of the year. It is an uncomfortable space, with nowhere to sit. You have to stand. You have to work out or remove a book and read. When you descend into this space, you have to improve yourself in some demonstrable way.

"You ready?" he asks, his Texan accent suddenly ever so slightly more perceptible, or is this a trick of memory now?

"Yes," the boy of my memory replies, and then his father punches him, not with even a fraction of his genuine strength but not in any way like a child of eight or nine, either. He throws straight jabs, repeatedly, on the chin, which astonish the boy, who has never been hit like that before. Has never been hit at all.

"You need to know how to take a shot, how to feel it on your face," Pappy explains lovingly but firmly, not jokingly, to the boy, whose mind has begun to race. "That way, once you're used to it, it can't ever take you by surprise." Stunned but determined to own the respect of his indomitable father, the boy nods his assent, wishing he were anywhere else. He withstands several more blows to the jaw and chin, the imprecision of the bulky gloves allowing one to graze the nose, flooding his eyes with salty tears.

The plane of remembrance shoots ahead and the mountain peak recedes; all that's left are the clouds. I have no more recollection of how that session ended, whether on a good or bad or neutral note. I know that Pappy never tried to teach me that strange lesson again, and I didn't ask him to. As it turned out, I never did muster the discipline to learn how to box. That is not to say I didn't learn, through trial and error, how to endure a fight. Rather, it's that everything I knew later to do with my hands, I managed from that day on my own, free-style—exactly the kind of life-learning my father despises for being unreliable and inexact. Even as a very small boy, then, I understood that Pappy was only showing me the sincerest kind of care. I understood that, for whatever the reason, my father could not relate, not fully, to anyone who hadn't experienced a certain amount of discomfort in life. And yet, I have always suspected that Pappy didn't like that lesson with the gloves any more than I did. I don't believe he really wanted me to ever *have* to rely on my hands.

BY THE TIME I was in the eighth grade, and had learned many things, including ways to harness whatever *otherness* I might possess, I'd scarcely felt more aware of my "race" than the times when I, in turn, found opportunities to terrorize Evan's sandy-haired little brother, who would never understand what he'd done to invite such hatred from me. That was also the year Pappy sat me down and presented me with my first serious choice over my future. I could either go to Delbarton, a school populated by salmon-pantsed Evans with competitive academics and an elite basketball team, a school we couldn't afford but where Pappy believed he could find me a scholarship; or I could attend Union Catholic Regional High School, about a mile down the road from where we lived, not particularly prestigious at all in either sports or classwork but gloriously, undeniably coed, with a student body that was not just white but equally black and Latino, too. At that young age, with untold pounds to accrue and inches left to grow, I still indulged my dreams of playing for a Division One college. But I didn't need five minutes to mull over my options. I told Pappy to sign me up that same day for Union Catholic. Part of this, of course, was hormonal—I wouldn't have gone to an all-boys school if my father had paid me to do it. But part of it was something else. This, I could tell even back then, would constitute the most meaningful assertion to date of my racial identity. I was black, and what I wanted more than anything else back then was to erase ambiguity, join ranks with the tribe my parents' style of life had mostly kept me aloof from.

Throughout my adolescence, largely spent on asphalt ball courts and planted in front of Black Entertainment Television—and because my father had severed all ties to the South, in the absence of flesh-and-blood extended black family—with what in retrospect appears a lot like the fervency of the convert, the zealously born-again, I consciously learned and performed my race, like a teacher's pet in an advanced placement course on black masculinity. Looking back, the sheer artificiality of the endeavor is what jars me most. The genes I share with my father, which have kinked my hair and tinted my skin, do not carry within them a set of prescribed behaviors. Everything I came to understand about being a "nigga," I absorbed on the fly from the contrived and punishingly Manichaean world around me. I use the word "nigga" deliberately here, not out of pride or even shame but matter-of-factly—while it represents ingested prejudices Pappy rejected, this is nonetheless what my classmates and I called ourselves, the defensive embrace of the way the Evans of the world already lazily viewed us—the superlative, in many ways, of what so many of us really did aspire or resign ourselves to be. This was how racial difference was made and compounded in my provincial middle-class suburb. Blackness, as I inhabited it and it inhabited me, was not so much what you looked like—that was often a *starting point*, but there is no more physically diverse group of Americans than "blacks." Rather, it grew into a question of how you spoke and dressed yourself, your self-presentation—how you *met* the world, the philosopher Martin Buber might say. Blackness was what you loved and what in turn loved or at least accepted you, what you found offensive or, more to the point, to whom your presence might constitute an offense. The 1990s will not go down in history as a particularly incisive political epoch in the history of black America. At the risk of overgeneralizing, when compared to the "woke" era we now inhabit, my generation's youthful apathy seems outrageous. My friends and I tended to favor form over content, the cant of a brim or the jewel in an earlobe; race pride for us could boil down to nothing more than rhythm and athleticism, the way a person learned or didn't learn to cut through the air; it was fussing over not looking fussed, the perpetual subterfuge of nonchalance. And yet, despite all that and so much besides, it was at its core *apophatic*, defined by what it was meant to lack. There are few things more American than falling back on the language of race when what we're really talking about is class—or, more accurately still, manners, values, and taste. This is why an older blue-collar Italian friend of my brother's could tell me foolishly but in all seriousness that my bookish pappy was "whiter" than his own financially secure but uneducated dad; and it's why a tough black boy I'd met could step inside our tiny house, glance at our shelves and in the cramped kitchen at my blond mother cheerily baking snacks, and declare against all evidence to the contrary, "Man, y'all are *rich*."*

ONCE I'D ADJUSTED to my new life at Union Catholic, I was able to find a girl who cut through the air just the way I wanted. I was fifteen, at the start of my sophomore year, when I noticed her in the hall most mornings as I rushed to class. She'd be strolling as if the bell were pitched to a frequency beyond her register. She was a year below me, fourteen years old, lithe, neither light nor dark but more of a polished teak, meticulous in her plaid skirt and navy socks up to her knees. She was rebellious, too, with unlaced construction Timbs and gold tangles of Gucci links around her neck. She blew balloons of pink bubble gum and rolled her eyes with feigned exasperation. She'd toss her hair, long with Indian weave, rolling those big brown eyes until all that showed were the bluish whites, and throwing her head back in shrill fits of giggles before seriousing up. She

---

* It is difficult to exaggerate or overemphasize the sheer amount of instances during my youth that my mother's cheerfulness alone, and nothing more than that, was earnestly conflated with "race," as if whiteness itself were really just the ontological manifestation of a good mood.

danced beautifully, like a woman not a child, and exuded a tremendous physical charisma in just putting one foot in front of the other. Even though she herself very rarely spoke meaningfully of her inner states, and seemed to me to live as close to completely on the surface of life as anyone I have known, she nonetheless exercised an incredible command over my waking mind. The way a weaker jogger will strive to match the pace of a stronger partner, I strove to meet her at her level of cool. The more time we spent together, the more I felt that Stacey made me whole—not just in the way that all lovers feel their beloved completes them, but literally: I was consumed by the idea of *increasing* my own physical and cultural blackness, of lessening any dilutions. She might have paid a lot to get her hair straight, but I would have paid more to make my own—which, when cropped close, grew in unbending needles from my scalp— coil as tightly as hers. In Stacey, I'd found the Platonic ideal of what would one day, in some distant, barely perceptible future, be my wife.

One rare unhurried afternoon, we stood together naked in the sunlight glancing off the mirror on her wardrobe, holding each other and luxuriating not just in the youthful, indulgent embrace but in the very image reflected back at us. Such proximity in those days was something furtive, hard-won, a thing stolen momentarily from the adult world, then always given back. In stark contrast to coupling later in life, there was seldom ever the chance to simply linger and *look*. But that day was different. She'd snuck me into her grandmother's house—I was foolish enough to go even though her grandmother was a corrections officer with a licensed firearm and a preposterously short fuse—and we had several consecutive hours alone.

When she turned to face me, her hand rested on my shoulder. Soon she began to giggle. "What?" I asked, still in a semi-euphoric state. "Nigga, what is *this*?" she cried, cackling, her thumb and forefinger delicately unspooling a single, impossibly blond strand growing straight out of my clavicle and limply falling over my left pectoral, shimmering in the afternoon sun. It was bone-straight and several inches long when fully extended, the only one of its kind I have ever found anywhere on myself*—nothing at all like the handful of white specks now infiltrating my beard— nearly translucent and very fine, the texture of spun platinum or Targaryen hair. I had never seen it before, but no matter how many times I would later pluck it away, it always returns, an irrepressible vestige of some Viking—maybe even Neanderthal—genes biding their time, waiting for the chance to reemerge. That afternoon we laughed hard at whatever it was my body was trying to say, and I left her grandmother's house perfectly content to think of myself as "black," albeit with a three-inch-long platinum-blond lock sprouting from my chest. I felt no inclination to return to the subject again with her or even in my own mind. We tend not to think about what is latent or in any way at odds with the idea of ourselves we are conditioned to project.

Today I often wonder what became of Stacey and think about the extent to which—already, by the age of fourteen—

---

* In adulthood I mentioned the existence of this solitary white-blond hair to my brother, who replied that he, too, has one, and only one, which grows directly out of his forehead.

she seemed to have been alienated from anything like an accurate sense of her own worth. I do not believe she knew what it meant to be loved, even by her family. Not provided for or lusted after but loved. I could intuit but never articulate concern over such distinctions back then. She did not come from poverty, by any means—I was acutely aware that her house was newer and larger than ours—but neither did she come from a nurturing place. Her parents were divorced and remarried, busy with work and distracted with their new partners and kids. She was lost in the shuffle and neglected as a result, common enough problems that don't respect barriers of color and class. But there was something else as well.

At the time, I could only lose sleep over the knowledge I otherwise buried deep and tried my best to disregard that Stacey reciprocated attention to many of the boys and men who pursued her, not just me. I've since come to understand that this doesn't really mean anything on its own—indeed, promiscuity in itself is neither empowering nor disempowering, it simply is—but even then I couldn't separate my knowledge of her own insecurities from my growing awareness of the extent to which many of my black male friends and classmates almost to a man seemed to derive their own self-esteem in large measure from an ability to move *away* from girls who looked like her. Most of them openly professed to want white or "Spanish"* girls to parade on their arms. For some of them, like my silver-tongued neighbor Ant, who frequented my basement to pump my father's weights and gossip after school,

---

* "Spanish" was a remarkably inexact term that almost never alluded to a person, or her family, actually having come from Spain.

this was, he insisted, because white girls as a category just tended to make for simpler conquests, and because a lack of life adversity (in his words, that internalized pain that springs from a history of having your families ripped apart, your men taken away and shipped off to the chain gang or the cell or shaped by life's harsh turns into something less than gallant) really did make them more pleasant. Their coddled upbringings left them unprepared for the type of misdirection girls like Stacey were conditioned to have to guard against (and, to be fair, frequently deployed themselves). Or, as my best friend Charles concluded: "Black girls just deal with too much shit, bro. I *get it*, but it's not fun." For other of my friends, though, and as I think about it Ant (though probably not Charles) would fit here as well, it would be hard to argue that there was not, on some silent level, the suspicion that white—or even just *light*—girls *were* in fact better than all of the girls who resembled their mothers and sisters—and *them*. (Their disproportionate approval of Puerto Rican or Colombian girls from even the most challenging backgrounds gave the game away.) These lighter-hued bodies were certainly a more effective indicator of their own status and worth. Even as a very young child, I could sense that this was what many people who did not know them would have assumed about my own parents' union—that this was what was really behind the hostile, incomprehensible, at times unseemly leers we attracted in Red Lobster as we passed through the dining room to get to our booth—and I resented and rebelled against that judgment with every molecule of my being.

Part of this has to do with the fact that, for as long as I can remember now, I've been stuck with the terrible image of my father being chastised by his own unloving aunt, commanded, really, when he was in high school: "Never to bring home a girl darker than you." It's a sentiment that is often but not always unspoken, rooted in dismal plantation logic, which, tragically, many blacks (and whites) would still recognize today even as it might appall them. Pappy never spoke to me about how my girlfriends were supposed to look, and he never shared this sad memory with me. He told it to my mother, who one day in turn relayed it to me, and it has pained me ever since I was old enough to contemplate a hate that points backward toward the self. I wondered why this black woman would preach the very same poison my white grandfather—who did not want his children bringing home people darker than them, *either*—would spew.

But I also knew the answer. In those days, I filtered the world through the veil of color W. E. B. Du Bois first taught us to think of as the "double consciousness" inherent in the black condition. Regardless of what you looked like—Du Bois himself hardly looked African—to be socially recognized as "black" meant understanding yourself on one level, as everyone does, simply as yourself, but on another level, "always looking at one's self through the eyes" of whites, and in turn "measuring oneself by the means of a nation that looked back in contempt." My father's aunt regarded his potential girlfriends—and possibly herself—through this hostile, foreign lens. I regarded *my* potential girlfriends through one that was inverted, coveting, and aspirational for homecoming, not escape.

When I arrived at Georgetown, I stuck pictures of Stacey around my dorm room like icons or advertisements for my own racial authenticity, and measured the new middle- and upper-middle-class black girls I encountered against her. I really didn't know what to make of them and found myself deeply conflicted in their presence. My fading connection to Stacey, coupled with a misguided understanding of myself as having arrived, however vicariously, in this rarefied space by way of a demonstrably tougher—read realer, "blacker"—high school experience, ironically allowed me to feel a degree of superiority over these young women. Like my childhood neighbors who thought that my father was "white" and my mother was "rich," I confused racial authenticity with behavior and taste and flattered myself to think that I was somehow *purer* than them.

Though I was the second one to notice it, by the time I came home from Washington that first summer after my freshman year, university life had changed me. Stacey, who had to my astonishment not even bothered to sit for the SAT test, graduated high school and stepped, like Wyle E. Coyote in those old Road Runner cartoons, off a cliff into free fall. We were now pointed in two different social directions, not because of genes or melanin or even because of material conditions, but simply because of a long series of decisions that we had made and that our families had made on our behalves. "Jesus, them white niggas got you buggin'," she scoffed during one particularly disastrous mall date when I bought a pair of dress shoes instead of sneakers. Soon after, she informed me that she was pregnant by a man who would support her with the income he reaped by selling crack. She moved out of her mother's spacious home and into the projects. I was crushed but finally resigned to the impossibility of keeping this increasingly untenable bond alive. In parting with Stacey I knew that I had also parted with that aspect of our interaction that I had for years now believed magnified my own blackness. I let go of the illusion that I was somehow more authentic than my new classmates. Yet what endured and even strengthened in her absence was my sense of myself as an inherently *black* man, and one who could only ever be complete alongside a woman who was "black."

In my second year at university, I met a girl different from any I'd previously known. Betrys was two years older than me and several color swatches darker on the Pantone scale, with an organized chaos of fluff around her head. The daughter of an Italian mother from Bolzano and a Nigerian father (whose real age she did not know and from whom she was bitterly estranged), she grew up in Manhattan, above Harlem, steps from the Bronx, and toggled easily between English, Spanish, Italian, and, by the time I met her, fluent Japanese. She called herself "black," and this was close enough to how she was perceived, though my father's kind of blackness—which was really a strain of Southernness—remained a mystery wrapped in an enigma, and she insisted that her immigrant mother, who came to working-class Brooklyn as a non-English-speaking teen, was not at all a "white" woman in the sense that my Protestant mother was able to be. We didn't use the word at the time, but of course what she meant was that in our society my mom was culturally "privileged"—and that this in turn *raced* her in a way that rendered obsolete any similarity between the two women's strictly physical traits, which were quite similar, in fact. At the age of nineteen, Betrys initiated me to the idea that identities are complex and even paradoxical things.

Betrys was cultivated, worldly, transparently honest, and full of self-respect. She evinced a cosmopolitan pan-African consciousness I'd not previously experienced,* quoting the Roots and Black Star lyrics, whipping up extraordinary feasts of *jollof* rice and fried plantains, and casually referencing the oeuvre of Chinua Achebe. She understood her blackness as a broad social, cultural, and political construct and she embraced it, cherishing and embellishing the connections and collective riches it engendered without ever seeking to use her links to Europe to shirk its hardships. But it would be impossible to accurately conjure her without emphasizing that she had one of the most specific self-conceptions of anyone with whom I have ever spent time. She was not mixed so much as tripled—fully an Italian woman who was also wholly Nigerian and ultimately entirely American.

But even that is far too abstract a description: Betrys was not simply Italian or even northern Italian, she was derived from the people indigenous to the Provincia autonoma di Bolzano—Alto Adige, or the autonomous mountain region of South Tyrol, whose capital is Bolzano, on the border of Austria. As a result, she did not see herself reflected in the foodways, mannerisms, or cultural practices of the many immigrants from Naples or Palermo who populated the Italian-American sections of New York and New Jersey

---

* My father is the kind of black man descended from Southern slavery, much like Albert Murray—but also like James Baldwin in his essay about African intellectuals in Paris, "Encounter on the Seine: Black Meets Brown"—who emphasizes the more incommensurate aspects of the black American experience.

any more than she did in their counterparts from Yunnan or Szechuan Provinces in China.

"That's *not* Italian," she would squint her eyes in physical anguish and whisper to me whenever we went to the deli in Carroll Gardens, Brooklyn, and some tired grandma would lop off the final syllables on *prosciutto* or *soppressata*. "It pains me!" she'd scream once we'd gotten our provisions and made our way back into the bustling anonymity of Smith Street, before pronouncing, in her own impeccable accent, every gorgeous letter of whatever word had sent her into a spiral of fury. This kind of distinction itself was a revelation to me at that time before I'd ever been to Florence or Rome. In the delis and pizzerias of my youth, I'd never understood the variety and—depending on where you are and who's doing the speaking—the transcendental beauty of the Italian language. In much the same way, Betrys was not "Nigerian," she was Urhobo, not to be confused with Yoruba, and the difference was as essential if not more so than the similarity.

I imagined that we would marry and have children who would inherit an enormous amount of ethnic diversity but inexorably mark the "black" box on any census or application. During the first phase of our relationship, our tentative plan was to move to Japan as soon as my studies were finished, and I would take a position teaching English and attempt to write fiction. Betrys had already graduated and was living in New York, when I spent the summer before my senior year in the Loire Valley, an hour by high-speed train south of Paris, struggling to complete a language requirement that was like a hex on my transcript. When I returned to Georgetown, I had one more French class to take in order to graduate and had, by this point, fallen in love with France as a country and even more so as a concept and as a context within which to come to terms with my own Americanness. But I had not yet gotten to know any French people intimately.

That all changed swiftly and unexpectedly. At this point in my life, I hardly even *saw* white women. I had nothing against them, indeed I was related to and loved more than one of them, but as potential mates they had—like many non-whites have in the eyes of whites—very little to do with my sense of who I was or who I aspired to be. Clotilde, an exchange student from Nancy, was immediately different. She was not a classmate. She was my class's TA. For forty-five minutes twice a week, she drilled her language into me. She was impossible to ignore as she looked me in the eye or turned her back and scribbled idioms on the chalkboard. She necessitated a response. Tall, blond, pink-undertoned, with a face that was nine-tenths dimples and wet blue eyes, she was almost the photographer's negative of Stacey or Betrys. But her very foreignness, her accent, her smell (Paco Rabanne plus coffee and Marlboro Lights), her—to my still-sheltered mind—astonishing political views on everything from Palestine to late capitalism, the manic way she chain-smoked at night, mittens flipped open to reveal fingerless gloves, it made her in my eyes somehow wonderfully knowable. In her exquisite specificity she ripped through the veil of color I had half-wittingly let blind me.

By Christmastime, absence had only made the heart grow less capable of communicating, and my long-distance relationship with Betrys had started to unravel. To my surprise, my passing acquaintance with Clotilde had so destabilized me that I did not fight to keep it together. As she and I began to date, I was at once wracked with guilt, feverishly liberated, and paralyzed by fear: for the first time in my life, I detected a fork in what had previously seemed a more or less straight and narrow path of identity. At the height of our time together, Clotilde cautioned that we were "parentheses" in each other's lives, lessons on the way to whatever we would become. Several months after I graduated, I found myself on a plane not to Tokyo but to Paris, with neither her nor Betrys beside me.

THAT FIRST TIME I really lived in France, some sixteen years ago to teach English in a depressed and depressing industrial town along the northern border with Belgium, I often went to kebab shops late at night in which I would sometimes, to my amazement, be greeted in Arabic, a language I had scarcely ever heard. The only Arabs I had known growing up in New Jersey were two Egyptian brothers who tried very hard to pass as blacks. One night, the young Algerian behind the counter simply demanded of me, "*Parle arabe! Parle arabe!*" and all I could do was stare at him blankly. "But why did your parents not teach you to speak Arabic?" he implored me, first in a French I hardly followed and then in an exasperated, broken English.

"Because I'm American," I finally replied.

"Yes, but even in America," he pressed on, "why did they not teach you *your* language?"

"Because I'm not an Arab." I laughed uncomprehendingly, and for several beats he just looked at me.

"But your origins, what are your *origins*?"

"Black," I said, and I can still see the look of supreme disbelief unspool on that man's face. "But *you* are not black," he nearly screamed. "*Michael Jordan* is black!"

Whites, too, outside of America—and even, oddly, white Americans while traveling outside of the U.S.—are just as often oblivious to gradations of blackness. I'll never forget on my first trip to Paris as a student during that summer study-abroad program, some classmates and I bought ice cream behind Notre Dame. When we sat at a table on the river, a white American tourist who'd overheard us speaking confessed he was homesick and asked if he could join us. He was very friendly and younger than we were, and I can no longer recall the details of what he'd said, but very quickly he got into an off-color joke about blacks. When no one laughed and one of my friends explained his error to him, he blushed deeply, and said by way of excuse that he'd simply assumed I was "Mediterranean."

Such failure to be *seen* as one would be back home was, of course, a major selling point in the previous century for a not-insignificant number of American blacks, primarily GIs and artists but other types, too, who found an incredible degree of freedom from racialized stigma here. Though, for many of these expats, it was not that the color of their skin went unnoticed; it didn't. It was instead that, even when seen, it carried a crucially different set of meanings and lacked others still. France has long functioned as a haven for American black people—and has never been confused as such for African and Caribbean blacks—precisely because, unlike in the U.S., we've been understood here first and foremost as American and not as black.* This, too, was a revelation for me—the sense that race was not something intrinsic and immutable but something fluid, illusory, and imposed, "an afterimage," in the British sociologist Paul Gilroy's words, "a lingering effect of looking too casually into the damaging glare" of conflicts and prejudices past. It is conditioned not just by *who* we are but—crucially—*where* we are. Like the adage about politics, *all* race is local. This makes sense given the basic biological reality that there is no such thing, on any measurable scientific level, as distinct races of the species *Homo sapiens*. Rather, we all make, according to our own geographical and cultural orientations, inferences about other people and ourselves based on the loose interplay of physical traits, language, custom, and nationality, all of which lack any fixed or universal meaning. It is this fungible aspect of personal identity that bestows

---

* The idea that genes translate into a stable racial identity or social reality is false. In a fascinating study published by *National Geographic*, scientists brought together dozens of genetically similar strangers "to begin to dispel the idea that people can be absolutely categorized into complete races." They settled upon six men and women whose DNA results "indicated essentially the same 'racial' heritage, in the following percentages: 32% Northern European, 28% Southern European, 21% Sub-Saharan African and 14% Southwest Asian/North African."

"We were just looking at numbers," said the molecular anthropologist Miguel Vilar, the Genographic Project's science manager. "They could look the same on a pie chart, and yet they could look very differently and would identify ethnically very differently and racially very differently."

"Despite this shared genetic past," the article explains, "each participant identifies differently, with some identifying as black, white, mixed race, or something else. If one looks at them as a group, the construct of race melts away, Vilar says, because the numbers don't translate directly to a racial identity."

From "The Surprising Way Saliva Brought These Six Strangers Together," Elaina Zachos, *National Geographic*, April 2018.

such a liberating (and at turns oppressive) quality to travel. Outside the confines of the United States, I was coming to the startling—and at times unmooring—realization that our identities really are a constant negotiation between the story we tell about ourselves and the narrative our societies like to recite, between the face we see in the mirror and the image recognized by the people and institutions that happen to surround us.

When I returned to New York after that year of teaching English in France, Betrys and I got back together and I mostly put these questions of identity aside. For the next four years, I fell back into an easy prefabricated idea of myself that did not require an enormous amount of scrutiny or skepticism. We were a black couple and saw ourselves as such—even on those occasions when we went out to lunch with our two white moms. It was an extremely complicated and willed simplicity that, for me, was a telltale sign that I was back home.

PART TWO

II

MARRYING OUT

N 2008, WHEN I WAS TWENTY-SIX AND STILL IN GRADUATE school at NYU, I received a moderately life-changing advance for my first book, a coming-of-age memoir. Though I'd worked feverishly for it—in retrospect, I had worked for it as though my life were at stake—the experience was like nothing I had anticipated. From one day to the next, I found myself with a sudden and expansive kind of freedom—up-front payment for work I would have to deliver in fourteen months. As soon as I finished school, I decided that all of my tasks were portable. It amounted to a genuine liberation after a series of personal setbacks. I was without a fixed address in Brooklyn—my relationship with Betrys had permanently come undone—and the act of writing a memoir meant that for large chunks of my days, I was living in my childhood memories. When I closed my laptop, what I craved more than anything was alterity.

I spent the autumn in Paris, borrowing a friend's tidy studio in the eighteenth arrondissement, behind Montmartre. I was under no illusions that I'd traveled to Outer Mongolia, but everything about life in Europe for me was nonetheless strange from the perspective of what I'd grown up with. Those were magical and intoxicating days. A Roberto Bolaño quote I underlined and copied into a notebook from that time gave the following advice: "Write in the morning, revise in the afternoon, read at night, and spend the rest of your time exercising your diplomacy, stealth, and charm." That is exactly what I made it my business to do. The streets of Paris, which I'd first encountered from a certain blissfully ignorant remove during my undergraduate years, were now unlocking themselves to me in adulthood and it was narcotic. I was no longer a student corralled in the tourist traps of the Latin Quarter or Bastille. When asked what I was doing here, I could reply, truthfully if not yet with total belief, that I was a writer at work on a book—*je suis écrivain*—a vocation that the French, unlike so many Americans, seem constitutionally disposed to value.

Those days, I searched for and did find so many things—in dining rooms, in passing faces, in friendships—that were, to me at least, entirely unusual. Better, I spent enormous amounts of time alone, wandering, daydreaming, studying, improvising, revisiting aspects of myself that I'd also somehow lost track of. Life was difficult in the way that lifting weights is—tension causes growth—which is to say it was rewardingly purposive. This was not New Jersey, nor was it even that cosmopolitan corner of Brooklyn I'd gotten used to, where career-minded young writers sit around and nervously compare agents and bylines until everyone is riddled with envy and anxiety; this was an old country in whose bustling capital you could stroll into a packed Left Bank theater on a weekday and catch Visconti's 1967 adaptation of *l'Étranger*, as if that were a perfectly normal thing to do. When a Swiss friend invited me to see the film with her, she made no assumptions about what I may or may not find of interest based on what my ancestors looked like. I was, I think, permanently affected by this sudden existential tabula rasa. Every movie, book, and conversation was potentially transformative, and I had hungered for new experiences. My expanding sense of myself and my place in the world happened to coincide with an extraordinary American political moment. When I returned to New York, I put my things in storage, moved to my friend Josh's couch, and volunteered to canvass for the Obama campaign in Philadelphia.

It was not the first time I'd volunteered. The previous winter, after he upset Hillary Clinton in the Iowa primaries, I felt myself overwhelmed by an idealism I'd never known before and cannot imagine ever experiencing again. It is almost embarrassing to recall today, but like so many people I knew at the time, I momentarily but genuinely believed that Barack Obama was the answer not only to our nation's depressing politics but to the question of our racial enlightenment. An editor that I met with while shopping my book half-jokingly suggested the title should be "Barack Is the New Black." It sounds unbearably premature now, but back then—at least in the section of New York I inhabited—Obama's (non-ironic) post-racial potential seemed undeniable and infectious. My initial reality check—in retrospect, that first intuition that the racial sickness plaguing our national life would require action on a far more collective scale—began on a cold dawn in Manhattan shortly before the mid-Atlantic primaries, when Josh and I picked up our friend Kaspar in a rented Toyota Corolla and peeled off southbound down Interstate 95. I had spent the night glued to CNN and poring over political blogs, too excited to sleep. Kaspar, a German investment banker from the Hamburg countryside, who, along with his very wealthy boss, became an exceedingly early Obama fund-raiser, and Josh, my Jewish best friend from college, were at least as captivated as I was. We didn't even stop for caffeine until we were past the Delaware Water Gap.

Four hours and three lattes later, we arrived at Barack Obama's Baltimore headquarters fired up and ready to go canvass the city. We were given clipboards, address lists, record sheets, and stacks of "Change We Can Believe In" flyers. What else could we possibly need? I thought, as we hopped back into the car and punched coordinates into the GPS. After a series of quick turns and a glimpse of Camden Yards, I made a right onto North Decker Avenue and eased to a stop in front of a beaten-down, boarded-up row house that seemed to slouch beneath its own weight. I felt a pang of déjà vu, as if we'd stumbled into a rerun of The Wire: blue-and-white Baltimore Police Department cameras dangled over intersections like sneakers strung from telephone lines; middle-school-age children stood lookout on their stoops, breakfasting on Cheetos and Pringles; jittery talk of last night's altercation drifted off the steps of the adjacent porch; two front doors bore the dimpled mark of the police battering ram.

We ascended a porch of unvarnished cinder blocks, and rang the buzzer. A heavyset woman in sweats and construction boots unlatched the door, positioning it defensively between her and us, like a shield on hinges, and peered out at the three of us. We told her we were hoping to speak with Jennifer about voting on Tuesday. "Jennifer is not home,"

she said. "But I'll tell her Senator Borama's people came by."
We thanked her.

When we began canvassing on the other side of the street, a shirtless man, missing teeth, his tattooed skin a camouflage of brown and emerald green, cut us off mid-pitch, calling into the house, "Ay, come to the door, the Jesus people back!" (The only white people we encountered in the neighborhood were roaming groups of missionaries.) "No, no," I explained, "we're not here for Jesus, but for Senator Obama."

"Who?" He squinted.

"Barack Obama," I said. "There's a very important primary election in Maryland this Tuesday, can we count on your vote?"

"I'm a convicted felon, feel me? Can't nobody vote in here."

I don't know why I was so unprepared for such a response. I looked to my clipboard for guidance. There was a box to check for "leaning Obama," a "Republican" box, a "leaning Hillary" box, and an "undecided" box. But there was no box to check for "permanently disenfranchised," and there was certainly nothing in my own personal experience that had familiarized me with it.

As we turned and left, the woman in the Timberland boots waved us back over like an airport ground traffic controller using a lit Newport Light as her wand. "Look, I *am* Jennifer," she admitted. "I just thought y'all was cops. Let me see what you passing out here."

I handed her a flyer, which she lingered over.

"Wait, hold up, this Borama guy, he's black!" she cried.

As we crossed East Monument Street, a shivering woman

in pajamas and a black overcoat shuffled past to purchase a vial of crack off some teenagers before dissolving around the block. We looked the other way. One of the dealers, a mere boy of no more than twelve, called over to us: "You wasting your time, yo, don't nobody live at that door there." We thanked him and moved on. We rang dozens more bells and were met with dozens more blank stares. We spoke to six- and seven-year-olds, who could not say, with any certainty, if in fact there was someone named Kenny who was living with them. We handed over our literature to an elderly man who smelled of beer and who, when he put eyes on Obama's picture, grew so excited that he ran into the middle of the street, shouting the good news at oncoming traffic. Minutes later, we saw the same man go back inside the liquor store, come out holding a brown paper bag, and proceed to get drunk. We saw many things—hope and change were not prominently displayed among them.

We wove our way back down to the car and came to a house where a slender young woman with long braids and an unzipped fly opened the door. She was topless. "Do you have a moment for Barack Obama?" I asked, forcing myself to maintain eye contact. She said yes and stood frozen in the entryway, glassy-eyed, listening, if it were possible to do so, in something like slow motion. A minute passed, perhaps two, as we made our strongest case. The woman smiled and nodded through it all, then glanced down—aware for the first time that she was naked from the waist up—and bolted to her bedroom. A moment later, she reemerged in a stretched-out red wife-beater.

"Well, can we count on you for Tuesday?" we asked for the hundredth time that day.

"Sure," she said, clutching her shirt to her chest. "What's on Tuesday?"

We decided to call it a day. As I returned to the car, dizzy with frustration, I remembered my mother once telling me that poverty, real poverty, was nothing so much as it was the permanent sense that nothing ever works. I was exhausted. My mother's words mingled in my mind with Marlo's from *The Wire*: "You think it's one way, but it's the other way."

When we got back to the campaign office, I slumped into a folding chair and began tallying all the responses on my clipboard. Another volunteer, a law student from D.C., sat down and asked me how the day had gone. "I would be surprised," I said, motioning to my friends, "if the three of us together are responsible for even three votes on Tuesday."

I asked her if her day had been different.

"Well, to be honest, this was a lot better than South Carolina," she said. "It got kind of depressing down there."

"This was better?"

"Yeah, I met a man in South Carolina who had never heard of the president."

"Wow, he had never heard of Bush?"

"No, he had never heard there was such a thing as the office of the president."

Now, as I think back on that excursion, I realize that no one I encountered on those Baltimore streets—some of whom certainly would have been able to perceive that I was "mixed" and therefore "black"—would have felt we shared anything particularly meaningful about our identities.

What would be the relevant and authentic grouping here for an outside observer? And what might seem contrived and artificial? A decade earlier, when Josh and I were with classmates in Belize during spring break, he made a passing comment about "gringos like us," to which I responded, "Speak for yourself, man, I'm not a fucking gringo!" He looked at me with momentary incomprehension but politely rephrased the same point as "college kids like us," which made all the difference to me. I had vehemently disagreed with his categorization then, and it took a lot more living for me to grasp the rationale. But that day in Baltimore it made some sense—or, rather, it felt undeniable. I was, for all intents and purposes, a gringo on those buckling porch steps, because amorphous, illusory concepts of race so often overlap with class and, really, with what is understood best as social or network capital. Do I really need to pretend that we are all united, socially indistinguishable, in order not to deny my African ancestry, to honor the experiences of my father's family?

Whether these men and women and children could read in my features a common essence that Josh and Kaspar otherwise lacked—whatever superstructural, sociohistorical latticework caught us together under a single expansive color category—seemed woefully beside the point given all that they were going through then and would inevitably continue to face. I am painfully aware that recent longitudinal research indicates that affluence and privilege remain far more tenuous for those deemed black than for those allowed to be white in America (or simply non-black), for a whole variety of probable reasons (some of which may or may not be self-inflicted and -perpetuating; that is another debate), with even the children of black parents in the top 1 percent disproportionately slipping backward or struggling just to maintain. From an intergenerational standpoint—and probably even for the comparatively brief duration of our own fleeting existences—I know that my position is statistically less secure than Josh's or Kaspar's. And yet, professional options, class distinctions and tastes, educational attainment, geographical mobility, and, perhaps as crucial as everything else combined, inner psychological wounds and barriers—or the absence of same—strike me as far more indicative of the shape of all those lives we encountered than the ethnic, national, or biogenetic characteristics that united or divided us from one another.

"What have I in common with other Jews?" Kafka asked in his diary. It's not the kind of question one is supposed to voice out loud. Of course, there were obvious social forces—and habits of thought—greater than any individual's control that linked him, whether he liked it or not, to many other men and women so designated as Jews in the society he inhabited. And he added this qualification: "I have hardly anything in common with myself. . . ." But none of that renders the initial query unworthy of serious consideration. And, while I recognize that members of "racial" groups will often broadly share aspects of outlook, culture, and tradition, it is certainly not a given.* I am sure

---

* Jews for Jesus, Candace Owens's "Blexit" movement, and the case of the "transracial" former NAACP leader Rachel Dolezal all immediately spring to mind as but a few of the more extreme manifestations of the limitless human capacity to surprise.

that I felt something grounded in my "black" identity—however socially constructed it may be—that Josh and Kaspar would not have been able to perceive on those surreal and heartrending Baltimore streets. But what, exactly, it is that I was attuned to—and what it necessarily should imply for the limits of my own life and personal ethics—is not so simple for me to relate. I say ethics because I am convinced—profoundly so—that what all of us feel we owe to each other must transcend narrow group identity and be rooted in values that strive to be universal (a loaded term in itself, I know, but still the best we can conceive) if it is to mean anything at all: I should not be more troubled by or connected to the plight on display in Baltimore than Kaspar and Josh simply because of the portion of my 23andMe pie chart that designates ancestry in Africa, or even because of whatever residual social conditioning I was subjected to through my paternal lineage. Nor, really, should Josh and I feel something fundamentally inaccessible to Kaspar merely by virtue of our shared American citizenship. Both are manifestations of the kind of deeply flawed but all-too-human tribalism that democratic, multicultural societies inevitably will have to discard if they are to fulfill their promise and potential. One way or another, we are going to have to figure out how to make our multiethnic realities work, and one of the great intellectual projects facing us—in America and abroad—will be to develop a vision of ourselves strong and supple enough both to acknowledge the lingering importance of inherited group identities while also attenuating, rather than reinforcing, the extent to which such identities are able to define us.

THE SECOND TIME I canvassed for Obama, he was well on his way to the White House. Josh—whose couch I was living on—and I took the BoltBus from Manhattan down to Philadelphia one Saturday and were assigned to some denuded blocks in Fishtown, the neighborhood that inspired a section of Charles Murray's book about the decline of the white working class, *Coming Apart.* This was the first and the last time I have ever seen what I can only describe as inner-city white strife, and it was just as eye-opening and foreign to my mind as what I'd seen months back in black Baltimore. The streets felt equally menacing, if not more so—whereas we were aliens in Baltimore, objects of mild curiosity or outright disinterest, here we were frequently objects of active contempt. To the painfully bored adolescents smoking and loitering on porches we were not harmless "Jesus People," we were embodiments of some vile and effeminate liberalism whose type they had likely glimpsed across town at UPenn or being pilloried on Fox News and had duly learned to despise. On their sneering faces, and sometimes in their belligerent words, we came to realize that these people—whose very lives and economic prospects were walking and talking proof of the diminishing value of whiteness as a racial category—did not interpret the arrival of a black president as anything resembling *progress.* A couple of the most aggrieved threw our flyers on the ground before we'd finished our spiel. Yet the neighborhood wasn't monolithic. There were others who did find Obama appealing. Usually these were women and older residents—working-class adults who reflexively supported Democrats for policy reasons, in whatever color they were sheathed. I will never forget the pathos of one obese, ash-blond woman in particular who opened the door with oxygen tubes strung into her nostrils, and amiably agreed to vote before pulling Josh aside and imploring him to help her keep her health care. She'd been laid off, she explained, and would soon lose coverage. "Will you be able to do that for me—can you ask Obama to do it?" I heard her request this of Josh in all earnestness, and her astonishing naïveté about who she was talking to and what he could possibly accomplish on her behalf left us both feeling stupefied with sorrow.

Days after the election and the pure euphoria that rippled through the streets of brownstone Brooklyn on the night of Obama's win—I am by no means the first to speculate that many babies (and no doubt a respectable "mixed-race" share) must have been conceived on November 4, 2008—I packed a suitcase of books and clothes and flew down to Buenos Aires for the rest of the year. I had no apartment, no network, no idea what to expect beyond blue skies, marbled steaks, and the opportunity once again to bury myself in my work. I had been initially headed to Mexico City, a place the idea of which I'd fallen in love with the moment I saw *Y Tu Mamá También* in college. That happened to be the last destination Betrys and I had traveled to together, where we'd holed up in Condesa for a few days before renting a car and driving west until we met the Pacific Ocean. I was eager to return, a desire that was feverishly excited by prolonged immersion in the writing of Bolaño, specifically his sprawling novel *The Savage Detectives*. That book amounted to a life-changing reading event for me, as well as further evidence of the possibility that a total stranger who checks none of the same identity boxes you do can nonetheless articulate your most ineffable aspirations and inner states more clearly than even your closest kin.

This kind of freedom to come and go was novel and exciting. It seemed then as it does today the one invaluable currency with which a writer might be paid. At the time of my arrival, I (barely) knew exactly two people to contact in the entire country. One was a slightly older novelist I admired who had cofounded the literary magazine where I'd interned and who lived what looked like an expat dream in a penthouse in San Telmo, the oldest barrio in the city, still full of tango parlors and exquisitely decaying colonial structures. The other was a slender brown-skinned girl with eyes so light they seemed to glow from her sockets. She had recently decamped from my neighborhood in Brooklyn.

I'd met Alana at dinner with friends four years prior while working with a classmate of hers from Dartmouth. The three of us along with another friend went on a kind of informal double date, even though we all may have been in relationships. It seemed to me then that our mutual friend had had the idea to introduce us simply because we were her two black friends, which is strange if you think about it even briefly. I still suspect this, though I don't begrudge her for it. Alana was smart, ambitious, dressed impeccably, and evinced a genuine vulnerability and sweetness. The truth is I did find her attractive that night for a whole variety of reasons beyond some common ancestral ties.

In Buenos Aires, I checked into a modest hotel while

foolishly expecting an apartment to materialize and English to be spoken in the process, as it might have been in Paris. (One did not, and it was not.) After several days, I mentioned my predicament to Alana and she made a swift intervention, helping me locate and negotiate a contract for a studio in Palermo. She was cheerful and thoughtful in the way my mother was and that I believed myself to be. Unlike Betrys or me, both of Alana's parents were black, but also unlike us, she was solidly from the upper middle class. She had none of that armor or scar tissue or callus or whatever metaphor my old high school friends identified as a condition of being black—a *racial* condition—but which I'd come to understand was really just a condition of personality and class. Here I was imagining myself adventurous and free, but it was Alana, in fluent, Barcelona-honed Spanish, who made that freedom happen. Maybe our mutual friend was doing more than stereotyping when she tried to set us up. Or maybe she was stereotyping on such a level that it was inexorably true. Now, if I imagine a computer matchmaking algorithm sifting through a list of all my friends and friends of friends, I don't doubt that it would reach a similar conclusion.

I worked well in those dedicated, sun-drenched weeks, rising in the morning and rereading *Anna Karenina* over breakfast at the nearest café. Afterward, I'd go home, weekday or weekend, throw the windows open, and write until late in the afternoon. Sometimes Alana and I would meet for lunch, but usually we found each other for a drink in the evening. After dinner we'd rediscover friends, mostly other expats or visiting Americans, then take a taxi to my bare-bones studio or her homey apartment. In the morning, we went our separate ways. Perhaps I was able to mimic the rhythms and intimacy of monogamy at that time because I always knew there would be a shelf life on the endeavor. My return flight was booked for the week of Christmas. I would stay with my parents in New Jersey and on Josh's couch in Brooklyn until I finished my book, which I liked to tell people was my only unbreakable commitment. I would not allow myself to return with a girlfriend, no matter how sensible that may have seemed.

Back in the Brooklyn neighborhood we both inhabited, Alana and I continued to run into each other, and sometimes when that happened I recognized what had been completely absent from our encounter in Argentina: the familiar weight of group pressure on my thinking. I could not have found a better black partner, a friend enthused to me when he saw her. I thought he was right, and told him as much, but what I'd prized about her was specific and sui generis. I felt no color qualification was needed, since we don't actually interact with groups or structures but with people. It was only in hindsight that I realized I'd become a statistic, a clichéd part of a much larger trend—the romantic game of musical chairs played out in a race-conscious society in which free black men's prerogative to take our seats where we please helps leave a disproportionate number of black women still standing.

I MET MY WIFE in a bar off of the Place de la Bataille de Stalingrad, in Paris. I was twenty-eight, and on that clear

January night, in a warm room overlooking the frigid canal, there was no one else, and I was accountable solely to myself. Valentine came with a mutual friend, slumped down catty-corner to me, and—who really knows how these things actually work?—something in her bearing triggered a powerful response. I found her insouciant pout and mane of yellow curls flowing over the old fur coat she was bundled in exotic. We hardly spoke, but before I left, I gave her my information on the chance she might find herself in New York, where I was living. Two months later, while there to interview the band MGMT, Valentine wrote me, and we met for a drink. That was when I discovered that she was funny as hell and not really insouciant at all, just shy about her English, which she'd picked up over the years from a combination of school and movies and childhood trips to the United Kingdom, where her grandparents had lived. The more we talked, the more it turned out we had a lot in common, above all a need to travel and a belief in the power of words and ideas, both of which resulted in a willingness to sacrifice comfort and stability in order to earn our lives by reading and writing. I saw her a second time a month later, again in New York, and then again on a work trip to Paris two months after that. Summer had just begun, and we fell in love extremely fast. When it was time to go home, she asked me to change my itinerary and join her and some friends for a week in Corsica. I did, and when it was really time to leave, she promised to visit me that August in New York.

A few days after she landed, we met my college buddy Jason for a drink. On a whim I introduced her to him as the girl I was going to marry. I thought that I was kidding, but the way she rolled with the remark, casually and confidently affirming that this was in fact who she was, amounted to one of those tiny little gestures that end up changing your life forever. A neighbor had given me the door codes to the building across the street from my apartment, which had a spectacular panoramic rooftop. After we'd left Jason, Valentine and I went up there for a nightcap, overlooking the Empire State Building and the rest of the electric-orange Manhattan skyline pulsating in the distance. I did not know that I would do it even twenty seconds before it happened, but when I got down on my knee and proposed without a ring or a plan, she accepted.

In the morning, I woke next to my fiancée both exhilarated and shot through with the terror I had only had a foretaste of with Clotilde. I was terrified because, as the saying goes, when you're black, you "don't have to do nothin' but stay black and die," with dying being the easy (or at least the nonnegotiable) part, and staying black a matter of some volition and therefore some character, too. Though it had been a long time since I'd thought in terms of having a *type*, the finality of actually having chosen a white woman felt anything but trivial. And while I now knew that it was impossible to marry or erect a future with "blackness" or "whiteness" per se, that knowledge did not entirely put me at ease. How could it? Overcoming such deep-seated fears is never strictly rational.

Of all the things in the world that lazy summer morning, I thought of Eldrige Cleaver, the Black Panthers' minister of information, excoriating a decadently cosmopolitan

James Baldwin for what he called the "racial death-wish" that motivates blacks to commingle with whites. In his 1965 collection of essays *Soul on Ice*, Cleaver rails against the "self-hatred" that runs so deep it "cannot be detected by the keenest observer, not by the self-hater himself." Was this not, after all, precisely what felt so repellent to me about my father's aunt's injunction to "never bring home a girl darker than you"—was it not, after all, precisely why I'd always promised myself I'd disobey her rules? I remembered Cleaver's famous, venomous allegory:

> According to Elijah, about 6300 years ago all the people of the earth were Original Blacks. Secluded on the island of Patmos, a mad black scientist by the name of Yacub set up the machinery for grafting whites out of blacks through the operation of a birth-control system. The population on this island of Patmos was 59,999 and whenever a couple on this island wanted to get married they were only allowed to do so if there was a difference in their color, so that by mating black with those in the population of a brownish color and brown with brown—but never black with black—all traces of the black were eventually eliminated; the process was repeated until all the brown was eliminated, leaving only men of the red race; the red was bleached out, leaving only yellow; then the yellow was bleached out, and only white was left. Thus Yacub, who was long since dead, because this whole process took hundreds of years, had finally succeeded in creating the white devil with the blue eyes of death.

Was I not, right now, all too gladly completing Yacub's sinister work—a racial murder-suicide, *wiping out* myself and my father's entire line along with me? The thought flattened me against the mattress. How long I spent on my back watching the ceiling fan twirl, I couldn't say. At some point, Valentine shifted to me and smiled, I thought, bravely. Perhaps she'd sensed my anxiety; perhaps she'd simply felt I'd been drunk from more than just love the night before and might not have meant all of what I'd said. "You know you don't have to go through with this," she whispered. "You have the right to change your mind." And with that, the material of my life was suddenly back in my hands, moldable in a way it seldom ever can be. I had a decision to make, and no one else could make it for me. I pulled Valentine closer, out of love, certainly, and also very likely out of something akin to stubbornness: I would not be bullied or reverse-psychologized—*You don't want to make Yacub's little white devils, now, do you?*—into forfeiting my own personal happiness and volition. What kind of liberation is *that*? I'd marry this woman I wanted to marry, I told myself, and all the rest was distraction.

When we arrived in New Jersey that weekend and stood over the island in my parents' kitchen to toast the news, there were so many unvarnished emotions on display in that room, it is dizzying to recall them now. Above all, there was the joy, the enormous joy a parent feels in recognizing the kind of love that creates and sustains families, secures future generations, which was illuminating both of our faces. What parent isn't overjoyed, after so many heartbreaks and false starts, to detect that at long last? And there was also the sober recognition—perhaps relief—that a phase of their own lives had now successfully concluded; their youngest child was standing on the cusp of thirty and leaving behind that decade of suspended millennial adolescence the existence of which had not been known in their generation when adulthood was held to be far less provisional. There was undoubtedly pride, too—they did not know Valentine yet, but they knew enough to know that this relationship was healthy.

"But has your father met Thomas yet?" my mother asked Valentine.

"Not yet, but he will be fine."

"What if he's not?"

"We will do it anyway."

I remember both of my parents being won over by this young woman's self-assurance. And I remember my mother's tears, which were shed through fits of heartfelt laughter and which she quickly wiped away. She couldn't say it, but I think she knew with a mother's intuition that, no matter what I told her to the contrary, this union all but guaranteed the imposition of an ocean between us. She recognized sooner than any of us, sooner than Valentine or even I did, that we would be moving to Paris, perhaps indefinitely. This sadness glimpsed on my mother surprised me only because I wanted to tell her and to tell myself that it was irrational. I wanted to insist that I didn't know what she knew: that a couple and eventually a family tend to move, like water finding lower ground, to societies and arrangements that present the least amount of resistance to their potential to flourish. My mother was not looking at a "black" man and a "white" woman standing there in her kitchen, as her own mother must have been doing some decades prior. She was really looking at two freelance writers, one American and one French, who could certainly use an easier environment to do all sorts of mundane, non-racialized things like secure affordable health and child care and find rent-stabilized space in which to live and work. The challenges she anticipated were not phenotypic—they were cultural, linguistic, and geographic.

My father's response was altogether different, though in retrospect as surprising as my mother's crying. Pappy does not hide the fact that he will always expect us to encounter racial resistance, if only more subtly now. *Did Valentine understand that a white woman marrying a black man in America would face stigmas?* She was unafraid, she assured him, and with that his reaction was uncharacteristically purely happy, with absolutely no qualifications. His levity struck and moved me deeply. This moment stands out to me still, marks the beginning of my adult realization of the blues-like stoicism and ambivalence Pappy has always held with respect to race and his categorization as a "black" man in America. It is his consistency that I most admire here—his willingness to hold two bitterly conflicting ideas in his head at once: *race is not real; race has harmed me severely*—regardless of the particular circumstances, and not to allow his own biography or history to dictate his children's. What I mean is that even though Pappy believes America is irredeemably racist, he refuses to be. It made no difference at all to him that

Valentine's complexion is "white," or even that his lineage would likely whiten, too. The man who told me years before that my WASP mother was just "light-skinned, with black consciousness" was not about to start fetishizing skin categories now. And if he shared my mother's concerns about our inevitable move, he concealed it. I think that what he saw between Valentine and me was a kind of freedom—a sovereign liberty to improvise and create the self without external constraints, which in truth he has always prized above just about everything. In this way, the black tradition my father belonged to was the open, omnifaceted one of Albert Murray and not at all that closed and spiteful one of Eldridge Cleaver: black American life, while certainly conditioned by local historical circumstance—and thus distinct from other strands of the African diaspora—was not *beholden* to it. It was a racial irony or ambivalence that would take me several more years to understand clearly.

TODAY, AFTER EIGHT YEARS of marriage, my path to Valentine seems obvious and irrefutable to me as an individual who has distanced himself from collectives and ideologies of all kinds and made choices as desires and opportunities presented themselves. Yet, none of our lives can ever play out in total isolation. What do we owe each other—not only those we're close to but complete strangers, too? Can "black" women, or for that matter "Asian" men—both of whom are, in contrast to the opposite sexes of their groups, statistically far less able to find partners of any race—meaningfully renounce their racial identity?* A part of me does, from time to time, still hear that indefatigable bully Cleaver: Why *does* it so often turn out that, when black men have the option to do it, we so disproportionately marry outside of the "race"? To this question, I have fewer answers than yet other questions still. Is it worth wondering what it even means to marry out of the "race" in a country where, on average, "black" Americans have approximately 25 percent European ancestry and are by definition an ethnically and even psychologically ambiguous, which is to say "mixed," population to begin with? And are we more or less likely to solve these problems through increased intermarriage and exposure to difference?

The truth is that upwardly mobile black men "marry out" so often it has become commonplace for scholars to describe black women—nearly seven out of ten of whom, like all of my black exes of all education and class levels, were unwed in 2010 when I got married and those figures were compiled—as facing a veritable "marriage crisis."† Even I'm amazed on a

---

* According to a 2015 Pew Research Center report, 24 percent of all black men marry non-black partners, whereas only 12 percent of black women do. Education exacerbates the divide. For black men and women with a bachelor's degree, it's 30 percent to 13 percent. By comparison, 21 percent of Asian men intermarry compared to a whopping 36 percent of Asian women (down from nearly 40 percent in 2008). Such gender discrepancies do not exist among whites and Hispanics, who intermarry at rates of 12 percent to 10 percent and 26 percent to 28 percent, respectively.

† In his 2011 book *Is Marriage for White People? How the African American Marriage Decline Affects Everyone*, the Stanford Law professor Ralph Richard Banks argues that black women, who disproportionately suffer from racial bias in the sexual marketplace, should nonetheless look beyond the black community, particularly in the direction of Asian men, for potential spouses. Many people could reasonably find such advice outrageously patronizing and dismiss it out of hand. But according to Banks, black women are half as likely as white women to be married, and twice as likely never to marry, while college-educated black women are more likely than any other group

purely observational level by the sheer frequency with which successful and often outspokenly race-conscious black men join themselves to non-black women. A few years ago, I attended a dinner thrown by the poet and novelist Ishmael Reed at the home of the tenor saxophonist David Murray. I hadn't previously known either of these men, but Reed was passing through Paris on his way to a book festival in the countryside, and he sent me an invitation along with a note on Facebook after having read an article I'd published. Less of a household name than Toni Morrison or Alice Walker, within the black community Reed is nonetheless one of the most esteemed living writers. I was deeply honored that he wrote me. I told Valentine about him and that I'd need the following Saturday evening. "Great!" she said. "Should we take a sitter so I can come with you?" I must have let the question hang too long or looked at her bizarrely. As I began to respond, "Sure, but you might be bored . . ." she blushed and laughed. "You don't want to *bring* me to meet your big important black writer, do you?"

The piece of mine that had caught Reed's eye was a lament about the toll in the age of camera phones and social media that the constant spectacle of extrajudicial killings

of American women to be celibate; more than 70 percent of black babies are born to unmarried parents; the majority of college-educated black women who are married have husbands who are not college graduates; and the racial gap in marriage rates between blacks and whites is actually vaster among the well-to-do than among the poor. Despite these sobering numbers, research shows a substantial majority of black women indicate that only black men are suitable romantic partners. They are less likely than any other minority group to express the desire to date outside their race. The cruel paradox of such tribal allegiance, according to Banks, is that it only *increases* the scarcity of marriageable black men.

of unarmed black men was demonstrably exacting on the collective psyche. I argued that, however much of a sacrifice it may seem, more black Americans might consider leaving the country. I'd taken criticism online—some of it hostile—for advancing what could be caricatured as an elitist, or insufficiently democratic, position. (*Yeah, cool, how is Michael Brown going to up and move to Paris?*) Reed's note felt like some sort of vindication. Here was a staunchly pro-black writer, a West Coast confrere of Amiri Baraka's Black Arts Movement, and a figure you can still find on YouTube chatting with Huey P. Newton—in other words, here was a man who could not be so easily accused of such transgressions—and he was cosigning what I had written. My reflex was not to want to disappoint him in any way. This was not only shameful, it was irrational: he'd have no right to be disappointed in my wife or in me for my romantic decisions, regardless of what he thought of my expatriation argument. I knew this abstractly, and I assured Valentine it was okay for her to come. Still, and to my surprise, it was something of a relief when it turned out she couldn't make it.

Beyond what I'd read and just assumed, though, the truth is I hardly knew anything about this man I was so happy to be meeting and worried about impressing. When the night came, I showed up at Murray's by myself, bearing the best bottle of Languedoc I could afford and expecting to be swept into what in my imagination would be an indigo-black scene, less "'Round Midnight" than neo–Harlem Renaissance on the Rive Droite. As I approached, I could hear the jazz riffs swinging through the hallway, but when I entered the apartment I was met by a white Frenchwoman who introduced herself as Murray's wife. (As it happened, he was away playing a festival in Switzerland.) She kissed me on the cheeks and led me into the living room, where Reed, a sturdy redwood of a man topped with a storm cloud of gray Afro, stood and gripped my hand. Then, in a commanding baritone, he presented me to his own wife—who, of course, was a white woman.

A person can never be reduced to a constellation of ideas or an intellectual stance, and I realize now that I had failed to extend to these men the same ambiguity in motive and taste I've grown accustomed to allowing for myself. Yet by the time I was seated next to a mutual friend, another older black expat writer from New York, and *his* white wife, there was no getting around the question of why it is so often the case that men like us, men who tend to be paid to think about and engage critically with the subject of race—from Henry Louis Gates, Jr., to James Baldwin, to Jordan Peele, to my own father, to countless others—*why is it that we have all made our lives with white partners?* Is this on its face a form of hypocrisy and even betrayal, as the Eldridge Cleavers and even the Spike Lees of the world would have us believe? Or is it possible that one of the most powerful and subversive ways—whether done purposely or not—to combat a racist society is simply to bow out of its perverse customs and mores, rejecting its false boundaries even as they work tirelessly to claim you? We tend to conceive of intermarriage in particular as almost exclusively a matter of race and to a lesser extent religion and class. But why must those be the only, or even the primary, categories of difference and similarity we measure and respect?*

I gradually began to condense all of these questions into the following question: Is "the only way to deal with an unfree world," as Camus ventured, "to become so absolutely free that your very existence is an act of rebellion"? That is exactly what the philosopher and artist Adrian Piper elected to do in 2012, when, after leaving the United States for Berlin, she publicly "retired" from being black. This was a provocative, performative gesture, of course, one that might strike many as foolish, naïve, irresponsible, futile, disrespectful, or some combination of all those things. But what if we took seriously the thought behind it?

"Retiring" from race, "marrying out"—these moves are not the same as "passing." Passing pretends to subvert but ultimately merely upholds the rules of an unjust game. Refusing to respect that game in the first place would be another matter entirely. But can you bow out by entering into an intimate relationship with someone designated "white" in a society that, even as it evolves to states of ever-greater inclusivity, nonetheless prioritizes whatever it perceives as "whiteness"? Does that really constitute an act of rebellion or is it in fact another form of capitulation still? These questions are exceedingly difficult to broach without flinching, and lie at the heart of so much anxiety over interracial dating and also "mixed-race" identity itself—"the persistent horror of the

---

* I know writers who are married to lawyers and have far fewer lived experiences in common than my wife and I do.

middling spot," as Zadie Smith, whose husband also happens to be white, has phrased it—and the prospect of a truly post-racial society that many of us claim to want to bring about.

THERE HAVE BEEN FEW ERAS in the history of the United States during which the racial malady of the nation, always lying in wait like Camus's plague, flared to the proportions of the late 1960s. On April 4, 1968, Martin Luther King, Jr., was assassinated (by a white racist) on the balcony of the Lorraine Motel, in Memphis. Three years before that, Malcolm X had been gunned down (by black racists) at the Audubon Ballroom, in Harlem. Los Angeles in particular and Southern California in general were still reeling from the monumental breakdown of social order that was the Watts rebellion of the same year. My mother had just graduated from San Diego State with a BA in sociology, after transferring home from Wheaton College, a devoutly Christian school in Illinois where she'd deepened her Protestant faith and forged a new identity volunteering in soup kitchens on the South Side of Chicago. President Lyndon Johnson's ambitious Great Society initiative was in full effect, and though she had intentions of pursuing a graduate degree, Mom decided first to put her idealism into practice. She took a position in the San Diego County War on Poverty program, in Otay—the same neighborhood as the conservative Baptist church where her father was the minister—and became the director of a center providing basic social and recreational services to low-income black and Mexican families. One evening, she hosted a community meeting and invited the executive director of the county agency to speak. As the fastidious Southerner (no, not "Southerner," he came from the Southwest, he would insist) standing before her carefully laid out his vision of social justice, my mother listened rapt, feeling as if he were speaking not just to her but *from* her, putting into words the inchoate jumble of thoughts that had been stirring in her mind for years, somehow speaking as an atheist words that felt even *more* Christian to her than her father's sounded from the pulpit.

The two began working together, and she fell in love with this man and his mission all at once, deciding that she would marry him. Nine years her senior, it took my father longer to reciprocate. He was wary of the ludicrous, irrational resistance he knew in his bones would be coming for them regardless of their intent. Only the year before, the Supreme Court had ruled on *Loving v. Virginia*, invalidating so-called "Racial Integrity" laws nationwide, yet Gallup polls showed the vast majority of Americans still opposed the idea that blacks and whites could marry (a staggering 72 percent to 20 percent). Justifiably fearful of compromising his position in the community and her relationship with her family and church, it was impossible for my parents to acknowledge each other romantically in public—an excruciating racial tax it boggles my mind to think they were forced to pay. It wasn't until my father accepted another appointment in Los Angeles, where my mother soon followed, that they were able to live openly and freely. After five circumspect years, my father proposed at last, once he was convinced that they were individually robust enough to withstand the ostracism and scrutiny they would surely encounter—especially once they decided to have children.

My father, of course, had already fled the stifling confines of his own social milieu in the segregated South. Because of job opportunities, but also, I imagine, because of his and my mother's need now to exist in a context of their own creation—away from the pain of her family and church's aloofness in California—they continually moved east until they were as far from San Diego as is geographically possible in the continental United States of America. As a result of both evasions, I grew up with zero extended black family contact and very close to zero extended white family contact, too. When I explained to friends and classmates that I had only a single cousin and she lived three thousand miles to the west, all of them, white and black alike, found this a pitiful absurdity. As a child I often wondered why I had no greater clan to claim for myself, though I knew from a very young age that I was unusually loved and prioritized within my nuclear family, and I wouldn't have traded such care and nurturing for another arrangement were the choice available. As an adult, I've come to further appreciate other, subtler advantages of being cut off from any substantial *we*.

The problem of racial difference in America—and in modern life more broadly—is always presented as an economic, political, biological, or cultural problem. But I want to say that it's at least as much a philosophical and imaginative disaster. We still struggle, in the twenty-first century, even to conceive of genuine and binding cross-racial ties. There are photos of my mother with the family that was hers before we became her own, which I have to scrutinize at length before I can recognize who she is. Who is this brood, with all that blond hair bleached a blazing shade by the California sky? One photo in which Mom is around thirteen years old, which would situate it in the late 1950s, finds her standing alongside her parents and infant siblings. Of course the children are just that, which is to say they are genuine innocents, but the parents inhabit a country that does not yet have civil rights, and they are posed in front of their new tail-finned Chevrolet with an unperturbed air that reminds me of something James Baldwin once observed about how racism dehumanizes us all but may in fact dehumanize the racist *more* severely. Looking at my Bible-thumping grandfather, whom I so markedly resemble in the facial structure holding up my tanner shell, several conflicting emotions well up inside me. I feel both anger and pity, but mostly I feel the cold unreality of familial connection. (I feel this, too, when I look at the old black-and-white photo my father keeps of his mother, whom I never met and who died when I was a toddler, and from what I understand did not think kindly of my mother.) It is hard to believe that we are in any way kin, any of us. In truth, we are "family" only in the most technical sense of the term. I feel no more bonded to this man (whose angular features live in permanent stalemate in me alongside Africa) than I feel to that sliver of pie chart on my DNA test results labeled "Senegal."

Nonetheless, he intrigues me. I neither love nor hate him. I feel sorry for him. And I wonder about the gratu-

itous charge he paid for having failed for decades to live up
to his own professed Christianity—even knowing that he
was failing yet unable to help it—by allowing himself never
to be bothered in any way at all with the all-American experience of someone like my father. To avoid that experience
at all costs, to avoid even recognizing its existence, to drive it
as far as possible from his mind and from his interpersonal
interactions, to curate his environment to exclude it, and,
finally, to be the type of man who when that experience
found him anyway would turn his back on it even as he
knew and could admit that the reason was skin-deep—what
then was the price, in real terms, of this clichéd, cookie-
cutter life he insulated himself inside? What did this Wonder Bread comfort and moral childishness cost him? I look
at that picture and my eyes wander away from him back to
my mother as I wonder why it is that some people *do* care
enough to get out of their own cotton batting, do dare to
lose their illusions about the unimpeachable moral rectitude
of the tribe to which they were born. Why are some people
able to imagine their lives beyond abstract boundaries while
others can't seem to do it? What is it that makes my mother,
with her inscrutable smile, staring off to the side, so different, so much braver, to my mind, than every other person in
that picture?

It is only now that I am the father of a daughter myself
that I can appreciate the exorbitant price of the loss my
grandfather did inflict on himself, and on my mother and
on my grandmother, too, but mostly on himself. Once a year
every autumn of my childhood, my grandmother, Esther,
would fly from San Diego to Newark and spend two joyful

weeks with us at our home in Fanwood. Two out of fifty-two weeks a year—not much in the grand scheme of things, but still that's all it took for me to love her profoundly, and for me to *know* her. I knew her face and her smile; I knew her smell and her long-legged stride that I moved double-time to keep up with; I knew the warmth and sweetness of her embrace and the gentle hilarity of her sense of humor and need to laugh. I knew without question that she loved me. During those two weeks, she was with me, by which I mean that she was genuinely present and took an interest in my world. She helped me with my difficult math homework during those two weeks, and she walked with me to the playground. She tickled my neck and concocted inside jokes that we alone could share. At the time, I never really stopped to question why Grandma always came solo. Why her husband forever remained aloof back home. "Oh, he doesn't like to fly," was a typical excuse. "He has a bad back, you know." These were some of the explanations that satisfied the child in me. I didn't think to ask myself why he couldn't call. Grandma, of course, made all the calls and signed all the birthday and Christmas cards for the both of them. It was only in adulthood, to my horror, that I realized what this absence necessarily implied. It was only, a few years before he died, while spending a month in San Diego at Josh's mother's house after graduation, that I realized how profoundly ungenerous— how impressively unimaginative—my grandfather's entire worldview could really be. I saw it then, suddenly and with the force of an epiphany, because for a moment the circumstances of the exchange had nothing to do with me.

By the time Josh and I visited my grandfather, who

really did have a terrible back, in the summer of 2003, he was confined to a motorized wheelchair and completely dependent on my grandmother, who seemed to work tirelessly on his behalf. A fire-and-brimstone kind of Christian, Grandpa was the type of man you could imagine, in another era, participating in—or at the very least vigorously approving of—an auto-da-fé. However, he could also turn on the charm when he wanted to and was in a wonderful and welcoming mood that day. He seemed genuinely to be proud that I had graduated Georgetown (with zero help or encouragement from him), and other members of my mother's family had come over that afternoon to visit with us, too, lending the gathering a festive air. My mother's baby brother, Bill—whom I hardly know but who also flew to New Jersey one summer when I was a boy and played volleyball with us in the backyard with such humor and goodwill that it endeared him to me for life (it's surprisingly not hard to show love to a child!)—was there as well. And so was her successful and worldly cousin, Walter, a man I met for the first time that day and have since grown very fond of in adulthood when he and his wife, Frannie, visit Paris in their travels. It was a deeply pleasant moment for me, that day, both a coming of age and a homecoming of sorts to a place that was only ever home in my imagination and my mother's retelling.

After Grandma cleared the coffee and snacks, and as Josh and I said our goodbyes and thank-yous, I regarded my grandfather in embarrassment and sudden disbelief as he wheeled himself over to a bookshelf and took down a crisp copy of the New Testament, pressing it meaningfully into Josh's hands. "I'd like to give this to you, son," he said. "I hope you'll read it with an open mind and think about it hard." I felt my heartbeat speed up. We had not spoken of religion, and we hadn't declared our ethnic affiliations that afternoon, so I still don't know how my grandfather discerned that Josh is Jewish—had he simply deduced it from the curve of his nose?—and I was too young or too shocked to express the anger that I felt welling inside me. Josh took the book and thanked him with an elegance it would have benefited my grandfather to learn to mimic. But as we drove away in pursuit of the Southern California evening, drove away toward the beach and other, lighter concerns, I remember thinking that I had at long last *seen* my grandfather for who he was. I remember finally feeling convinced, and perhaps on some level vindicated, too, that this smallness *was* him. But it wasn't him alone. He was simply exercising—explicitly—the prerogative of many men and women just like him. This was the arbitrarily normative nature of my grandfather's WASP identity—the false universality of his own tribal bias—put into appallingly hierarchical practice. Were there a book that could have converted my father from his blackness, I have no doubt in me that my grandfather would have procured a copy and magnanimously slipped it to him.

MORE RECENTLY, my aunt Shirley, my mother's baby sister who is the relative I am closest to, someone I love very much and who is also something like the family chronicler on Facebook, posted an image of an ancestor I'd never seen or heard of before. The purpose of her post was to wish her maternal great-great-grandfather, Anton Spath, a happy birthday. Born in Dietzenbach, Germany, in 1835, Spath, who had been a weaver, immigrated to Baltimore in his early twenties. He married a woman named Anna, and the couple's first child, Anton, Jr., arrived the year before the Civil War concluded. Anton Spath managed to buy property on which he grew willows for making baskets, tended a small farm, and sold rock from his quarry. As the opportunities presented themselves, he bought other neighborhood houses at auction. Anton Spath had amassed some twenty rental houses on Spath's Lane, Oakdale Road, and Falls Road at the time of his death in March 1913.

I stared at my aunt's post for a long time. The way my aunt and members of the family talk about it—indeed, the way many, many white Americans talk about their immigrant forebears—is to talk admiringly of men and women rising through thrift and tenacity from humble European origins to prosperity in the New World. In a sense this is certainly true. I am deeply impressed by what this Anton Spath was able to accomplish as a German-speaking basket weaver in Baltimore. And yet those *dates*, and the innocence with which they are recounted now, tear at me, too. I cannot help but know that at the same time Anton Spath was amassing his property and enjoying, as a *total* foreigner, all the power, dignity, and security that come with that ownership, my father's people—many of whom had been in America for many generations before Spath was born and could trace their ancestry to both Europe and Africa—were enslaved not so many miles away.

Before I made the decision to spit into a vial in exchange for an email containing the results of my DNA, I spent several maddening weeks on the website Ancestry.com* erecting the sparsest of paternal family trees. Williams, Welsh in origin and the third most common surname in the U.S., is an almost meaningless starting place, as far as these quests go. (Years prior, when handling a bureaucratic matter in Brooklyn, I was told that there were not only some eighty-odd other men by the name of Thomas Williams in my zip code, there were some eighty-odd by that name *with criminal records*.) My father's mother's maiden name, Mclemore, is only somewhat better. The farthest I can trace that name back is 1865, the year my father's maternal grandfather, James "Pump" Mclemore, was born (an exact contemporary of Anton Spath, Jr.), perhaps in Mississippi, perhaps in Texas—in either event, right on the knife's edge of bondage and liberty. Before that, there is simply the void, an endless abyss of inhumanity from which names and dates seldom emerge.

Among the very first blacks in the U.S. to be born into emancipation, Pump Mclemore (who apparently got his name from a fondness for the pump organ) was, improbably, a literate landowner by the time he married my father's grandmother Cora Jones, herself a descendant of Louisiana slaves. Most of what I know concerning this ancestral first

---

* The technology is far from perfect or satisfying, but it can still be awesome. After I spent hours tunneling down the genealogical rabbit hole, one brief, incredible, and totally unexpected joy was to find myself seated at my dinner table in Paris, suddenly staring at the actual tombstone of my father's grandmother Cora (from whom Marlow received her middle name), so tangible and real all those many thousands of miles away in Texas.

man comes from a 1910 census form I was able to track down on Ancestry.com (my heart swelling when I noticed the "Yes" box marked with his own hand beside the query "Able to read?") and from the few anecdotes Pappy has inherited and preserved from Cora ("After long days of grueling farmwork, he used to like to float in the Caddo River, where it cut through his property, and sing). Neither my father nor I have a clue as to what this man might have looked like, or how on earth he managed to buy any land. What I do know is that he and Cora, sixteen years his junior, had eight boys and girls, before he left her a widow for the majority—perhaps the duration, we don't yet know when he died—of my father's mother's life.

Until recently, I'd never even seriously thought about investigating my ancestry or pressing my father for clues. He'd volunteered scarcely anything on his own concerning the generations preceding his mother, perhaps because it is so painful, and perhaps again because in his time black kids who grew too inquisitive were duly told to keep quiet. That's what his family often said to him, and it was good enough for me until Marlow was born. It's been her presence that made me yearn for a better response now. It anguished me to think that she will chart her French side for centuries, not because the history is so illustrious—indeed, one of her paternal great-great-grandfathers, whose factory had been forced to supply the Nazis, was deemed a collaborator after the occupation—but simply because it's *there*, tangible and contiguous, for all to see. Yet this black kernel of identity, which I'd grown up believing was potent enough to infuse anything it touched, loses its coherence at such a remove.

On the 23andMe website there is a disclaimer that the knowledge will be "irrevocable"—in addition to information about predispositions to genetic disease, one can imagine that warning being put in place for the 24 percent of white Americans liable to find some unsolicited sliver of Africa in their pie. After all, as the artist and philosopher Adrian Piper has noted, "In this country . . . the fact of African ancestry among whites ranks up there with family incest, murder, and suicide as one of the bitterest and most difficult pills for white Americans to swallow." The reason for such aversion, however scientifically insupportable, is hardly difficult to understand: to be white in America has meant to be descended from liberty and a modicum of dignity even in penury—even when you wash up on the shores of Baltimore, Maryland, a German-speaking basket weaver with scarcely a deutsche mark to your name. On the other hand, to be black has meant, more than it has meant anything else, to be irrevocably stigmatized by the inhumanity of chattel slavery—like the tragic virgin in a traditional society who through no fault of her own is violated and then, because of nothing more than the violation she has endured, finds herself permanently ineligible and scorned. These essentialist terms by which our thinking about race has operated for so long, mutable as they may be, are rooted most powerfully in a crude distinction between people who are perceived to be defined by an inherited condition of inferiority and those who are not.

Still, despite the taboo, racial boundaries have never been impenetrable and are more porous today than they have ever been before. We no longer make of interracial relationships what we once did—at least not when the more pressing questions of class are answered to a satisfactory extent. I didn't know what to expect when Valentine and I took the train from Paris to Brittany to tell—not to ask—her father about our engagement. But I knew that my dignity was not at stake. Perhaps this is because I am light-skinned, perhaps it is because I could reasonably expect to be understood in Europe first and foremost as American and not as black, or perhaps it's simply because were he to object to my race, it would have scant impact on my self-conception and sense of comfort in the world. Unlike in my father's day, I could expect that society would not reinforce his limited vision of me everywhere else I might turn. This shift, this diminution of the anathema—if you can accept it—makes possible a degree of magnanimity even in the face of bias and hate.

But there was no need for me to be magnanimous the evening I met Valentine's father in the backyard of the house he rents each August, overlooking the incessant drama of the bay of Saint-Malo, where the tide comes in and out to such an extent that you can walk a mile from the shoreline when it is low. Midway through dinner, we made our announcement, and his reaction was to leap from his seat and embrace me, kissing both of my cheeks, before immediately directing his youngest daughter to book a table on a local terrace so that we could continue to celebrate with champagne. I have often contrasted this normal and decent response with the unthinking brutality my grandfather directed at my father, and it leaves me both sorrowful and optimistic.

In my own marriage, I've come to realize that I seldom if ever experience the kind of painful division I once felt so sharply in the grocery store checkout with my mother, when that white woman glared at us and so easily assumed that we couldn't be kin. Again, this has a lot to do with the fact that the world is much more used to mixing today than it was even three decades ago, and it has to do with the fact that we have always lived in cosmopolitan cities, but it also has something very much to do with the fact that people are more than a tally of physical, national, or ethnic characteristics. Valentine is a soulful girl who can dance and grew up steeping herself in black music—some of which she has introduced to me for the first time—but not in the attendant American mythologies, while I am a longtime student of France, still capable of surprising us both when I reveal to my wife an aspect of her country or literature she has not known. We do not have much inherited shorthand for each other, and this has been a gift, forcing us to learn each other from the ground up, as individuals instead of ambassadors of race. Our marriage is hybrid in so many more meaningful ways than, say, the textures of our hair. And yet, I would be a fool not to think that my wife's hair—and especially her eyes—does continue to carry more value in our society than mine. This is why strangers, almost always well intentioned, would stop us on the street to exclaim, *Ooh la la, les beaux yeux bleus!* when they saw our infant daughter. In retrospect, it is why my high school best friend Charles took to wearing colored contacts for a spell, and if I am honest, it is why even I found myself wondering inordinately, before she was born, whether or not Marlow would have Cleaver's coveted "blue eyes of death." But this is precisely the kind of bias it is in my power to, and that I must, reject—while being mindful not to fall into the trap of resentment—for it is with such minor and arbitrary preferences that entire worldviews are sustained.

Like any parent, I'm wracked by a host of generalized fears for the well-being of my children, but I don't know that very specific angst I've seen streaming down my Facebook and Twitter feeds for the better part of Obama's second term and which has only intensified under Trump; that sense of being under permanent siege that many of the black parents I know—all the way up to those employed at hedge funds—have voiced since Trayvon Martin was killed. A few summers ago, dozens of these parents circulated the video of a white police officer at a community pool outside of Dallas dragging a fourteen-year-old black girl clad in nothing but a bikini to the ground and then kneeling on her back, his weapon trained on whoever might come to her aid. Even as I share their outrage, even as I remain aware that this could still happen to me, I know as well as I know my own name that this is not one of the things I need fear could happen to Marlow. How can I deny that there is a part of me—a real one—that feels relieved; and how could this relief in turn not look a lot like treason?

And so there is still that stubborn question: Given such a context, is it unethical for black people to date, marry, and procreate outside of the "race" instead of strategically banding together? This is a conundrum made all the more pressing in light of the country's current demographic trends. With the one-drop custom I was born into now at long last on the wane, could the rise of a comparatively privileged, white-beige population (including ever more Asians, Latinos, and further decreasingly "black" mixtures), unburdened by such concerns and—as technical minorities themselves—impervious to accusations of "white privilege," result in a stigmatized, dark-skinned population's further neglect? Or is it possible that marrying out, if shorn of any belief in or aspiration to "whiteness," could be a useful, even indispensable part of the solution to the quagmire of racism without race? The answer to all, I believe, is, *Yes.* Given that, and the cost we know of maintaining the status quo, what are we to do?

PART
THREE

‖

SELF-PORTRAIT OF
AN EX-BLACK MAN

A T EIGHTY-FIVE, GENEVIEVE, THE WIDOW OF VALEN-
tine's paternal grandfather, is a hardy, imposing
Parisienne, brought up in boarding schools and with ser-
vants and a general sense of ownership in the world that,
for reasons of race and class and demographic shifts result-
ing in competition for resources on a global scale, neither
Valentine nor I will ever know. As a child, she played and
danced ballet with Brigitte Bardot. There is a documentary
that sometimes airs on French TV that shows a photo of the
two as teens, coiffed and pirouetting together, rehearsing for
a charity recital at the Théatre du Chatelet. It's a beautiful-
looking life, even all these years later. Once every month
or two, Valentine and I, now with Marlow in tow, make
the ninety-minute trip to her home in Normandy, where
we were married and where many of Valentine's formative memories were made. The place is remote enough that
there are no numbers on the address, just an intersection of
narrow roads winding through the apple orchards and horse
and dairy farms that crop up along the region's *route du cidre*.
As often as not, the names of the little towns and villages
along the way are familiar because of their excellent cheeses.
This property has always been Valentine's oasis, one she is
understandably eager to impart to Marlow while the family still has it. (It is not something the next generation will
be able to maintain.) There is an old main house, part of

which used to be an apple press, a guesthouse, and several small outbuildings all done in the gnarled *colombage* typical of the region; and there are wild fields, ponds, a rolling lawn, and, for the rare days it's warm and sunny, a swimming pool tucked into the hillside, surrounded by a jubilant garden of flowers Genevieve is a master of bringing to vibrant bloom. It's not a lavish home, but the plot is the size of the municipal park I spent my summers in as a child in New Jersey. I am certain that besides myself and Valentine's cousin's high school boyfriend, the only black people to have set foot on this land came as guests to my wedding.

Genevieve was fourteen when Nazis and later Americans seized her own family's property in Normandy to quarter their soldiers. Like my father, she's lived in a world I can't fully envision. Her brother was killed just weeks after enlisting in the war, and she has told me it got so bad at times that she may have once eaten human flesh. And yet, when the fighting was over, her life more or less resumed as normal, back to the country clubs and back to her place in the lower reaches of the upper tier of a European society that still held an immense global network of colonies and influence. When I met her, even after I had met Valentine's father, I really didn't know what she would think of me, either. A woman of her generation, reared in a culture that was many things but certainly not diverse—it wouldn't have surprised me if she were cold or standoffish. The fact that she wasn't, that we'd taken to each other almost immediately, with her making me at home in Valentine's home, was not exactly a surprise—after all, I'd given her no reason not to, and unlike when many black Americans deal with whites, this really is the default way I expect to be treated—but again I wonder why it nonetheless seems normal for me to give her *credit* simply for accepting me.

In spite of—or really *because* of—this easy acceptance, I am often thinking about skin when I'm in Normandy. Valentine, her younger sister Juliette, and I rush into the yard to sunbathe at the first rays of light to puncture the heavy skies; Juliette, whose mother's family is from the south, near the Spanish border, gets several shades darker than I do, and this is a source of amusement for us both. Marlow is the palest person in the family by a standard deviation, and Valentine and I are preoccupied with preventing her from burning. And then there is that glistening dark brown skin of the face peering at me from the table. It never escapes my notice that among the muntjac antlers and equestrian prints—little anachronistic emblems of mastery—Genevieve keeps an astonishing, thick-lipped, bug-eyed porcelain head of a slave or servant woman on her coffee table (lidded and hollow inside, meant to hold bon-bons, keys, and other knickknacks). Whenever I am in the living room where this keepsake is displayed, I am incapable of denying it my attention.

The first time I saw it, we'd just come in from swimming, and I was on my way to the bathroom to wash up before lunch. When I came back and sat down, I wanted Valentine to tell me I hadn't seen what I thought I had. She blushed. We ate the mounds of shellfish Genevieve put out, followed by the customary local cheese, and I thought of other things. But when I took my coffee to the sofa, I could feel that cursed head's eyes glued on me, watching, judging, maybe even imploring me not to forget. Valentine and her cousins often hide the head when their grandmother isn't looking, but sometimes there is no clear and diplomatic way to do this, and I never insisted, though I have asked myself if this alone is enough to mark me as a traitor.

I wouldn't be able to explain to Genevieve why I don't want my daughter to see this object when she's old enough to grasp its historical implications. She'd be mortified, I know it, but I'm also under no illusions that she could truly appreciate just what about this souvenir poses such an existential problem for me. Valentine does, and I've complained at length to her, and yet the bizarre thing is the more I complain, the more I realize that I am also playing a role, willing myself, even, into some strange communion with an anger that exists somewhere outside of me—an anger that has never rightfully been *my own*. The lived experience behind the anger belongs to someone else, to a memory. My wife and I can argue until we actually begin to laugh at my torment, because the grievance remains too abstract, too artificial. Of all the things I feel, I do not feel myself to be a victim—not in any collectively accessible way. Try as I might, I do not see myself—or my father or anyone else I know and love, for that matter—in that sad porcelain figure. And so I am left to question just why I am bound and defined by this sordid past in some *truer* way than I am allowed to be by my more or less leveled present (perhaps it is less than level, but what life is perfect or wholly commensurate with any other?) and my daughter's as-yet-unwritten future.

What I do know is that it can come almost as a relief to members of historically oppressed groups when they do find evidence of bias or insensitivity: *What did you think?* Of course *she keeps a woolly-haired slave's head on her coffee table!* the logic goes. Racism—like "race"—will always be what it's always been, we tell ourselves, and there can be no exit or respite. Might as well wake up, then! Wake up and *get out.* "It is easier to believe that the world does not change," Leon Wieseltier observed about anti-Semitism, "than to believe that the world changes slowly." Yet the wound can and does heal; I have seen this. That slave head in its terrible specificity is troubling, but the conclusion I draw from the greater dynamic of all of our lives assembled there in Normandy is far from pessimistic, since the terms on which people like Valentine and I meet and live with each other have been (and will continue to be) powerfully altered, and since we really have created—*right now*—a mixed-up and imperfect but thoroughly accepting and loving family. What I am most acutely aware of are those tangible moments Genevieve has interacted with my flesh-and-blood father, how warmly she has hosted him and my mother, and how she asks after their health at every turn. I do not, and do not wish, to see myself in the master, but can—and *should*—I really claim to glimpse in the slave's face my own eternal reflection?*

---

* The situation I have just described, in today's academic and social media discourse, would solidly qualify as a "micro-aggression." According to Derald Wing Sue, the professor of psychology whose work popularized the term (originally coined by the psychiatrist Chester M. Pierce), micro-aggressions are "the everyday verbal, nonverbal, and environmental slights, snubs, or insults, whether intentional or unintentional, which communicate hostile, derogatory, or negative messages to target persons based solely upon their marginalized group membership." Genevieve's warmth toward me and my family is significant and matters quite a lot to me personally, but it is true that this is merely a particular interaction and the porcelain head exists as part of a larger matrix of demeaning imagery of black people—regardless of how she treats me and whether or not she intends it. This is a residue of more

———

SEVERAL TIMES A YEAR, I speak at universities about my first book, *Losing My Cool*, which draws a personal picture of the influence of the street on black youth culture. Since marrying Valentine and moving to France, and especially since the birth of Marlow, I find it harder and harder to deliver the talk that as recently as 2010, when the book was published, felt so inextricably linked to the very core of my being. Partially this is because for a spell many of my lectures began taking place at historically black colleges where the kind of hip-hop culture I am critiquing but no longer participate in (in no small measure because of age) is simply the air my teenage audiences breathe. But partially it is also because my "black" experience has veered so drastically and demonstrably from their own.

On one such occasion in Florida, I met with a small class of freshmen before my university-wide talk. During the back-and-forth, a dark-skinned boy with handsome, meticulously twisted dreadlocks and an inscrutable mien asked me almost in a whisper why white people "hate us so much." Other than myself, I don't think the question took anyone in the room—including the worldly professor of media

———

flagrant racism that is very difficult to stamp out and that can often be internalized by whites and blacks alike, to the detriment of the latter. However, the only question in my power to answer is, "Are you going to let this harm you?" Ultimately, my wholehearted response is: "No, I'm not going to allow it to harm me." As we continue to work to create—and in fits and starts really do more fully realize—a world beyond race and racism, there will be incalculable small, unfortunate situations such as the one I have recounted, instances of micro-aggression brought about in liminal spaces between the racist past and a more perfect future. They can either be seized on and blown up or deemphasized whenever possible. To do the latter, it's inevitable that someone will have to make the first move. I am more committed to getting to that more perfect future than I am to always moving second.

studies who presided over the conversation—too much by surprise. As I struggled to meet him with a sufficient response, I was struck by the thought that this young man, like many of his peers who nodded in agreement, like many blacks of all ages across income and education levels nation-wide, like my own family in Texas must have been before my father revised the script, had probably never intimately known or loved a white person—and he had probably never been known or loved by one in return. All I could think to tell him was that while there are certainly racists to guard against, I don't believe that most white people *actively* hate black people; the truth, in my experience, is less dramatic: Most white people don't or cannot think very seriously and with adequate nuance and stamina about black people at all. And they lack the imagination or will to try.

Such de facto segregation and mutual alienation damages all of us, black and white alike—as James Baldwin and Martin Luther King and many others have eloquently pointed out, it denies the former humanity while rendering the latter inhuman with indifference—but it hurts black people more, no matter how much I want Baldwin's counterintuitive point about my grandfather to be true. I've been granted a view that most Americans on either side of the color line haven't had, but from a position that an increasing number will find themselves in as the mixed-race population expands. And while I've benefited from this view, it is true that it has come at a price—namely the terrible realization that so many people are unreachable and won't allow themselves to be reached—which is perhaps never more acutely felt than when I am privy to the mechanics of what for want of a better term I'll call the privilege to be oblivious.

THE SUMMER OF 2014 was a time when many of us grew accustomed to a new kind of spectacle. Viral videos of black men (and children) in the throes of death invaded our smartphones and computers. We consumed these images, whether in a state of rage, indulging a morbid curiosity, or scrutinizing the moments before and after for evidence of that thing that could maybe, just maybe, make the loss justifiable. Different cases, and their legal outcomes, struck different chords. For me, the refusal to charge Officer Daniel Pantaleo with even negligent homicide or manslaughter in the documented killing of Eric Garner, a nonthreatening man selling loose cigarettes on Staten Island, combined in my mind and conscience with the unpunished split-second execution in Cleveland of Tamir Rice, a twelve-year-old armed with a toy pistol. All the other abominable slayings accumulated on top of these and provided me cause for a lot of sadness and reflection.

After the Staten Island verdict, Kris, a close photographer friend who is also black, and I decided to proceed with a project we'd talked about since the previous summer. We launched a Tumblr account to compile the oral histories and portraits of as wide a variety of black men as we could reach. Our goal was simply to do whatever little we could to complicate what is still far too often a tragically basic understanding of what it means to be "black" and male in America. We made a call for submissions on

Facebook and, as would be expected of something like this, received plenty of positive feedback and encouragement from friends of all colors. It all seemed rather innocuous.

But then at some point my twenty-year-old white cousin Hope, with whom I've only ever really exchanged banter and small pleasantries, inserted herself into the thread on my page, angered and challenging the worthiness of our desire even to tell these stories about black men in the first place. "Will you be doing one with white people?" she asked. "Maybe a long time ago the life of a black man would have been considerably different at no fault of their own . . . but now I believe if the life of a black man is any different than any other person's life it is their choice and their doing. Your skin no longer defines who you are unless you let it."

My cousin has always lived in the Valley of Los Angeles County. We've only seen each other a handful of times. For all intents and purposes, she is a stranger. I can't claim to know her soul or even much practical information about her. But from the contours of her biography that I do know, in probably every single important way her life has been *much* harder than mine. Still, by all accounts and impressions, including my own, she can be a sweet and caring if willfully ignorant, myopic, and provincial girl. I saw her last at my brother's wonderfully mixed-up wedding in upstate New York. He's friendlier with her since they'd recently bonded in California over off-roading, poker, and talking about the NFL. I know that my cousin likes my brother and would even say—in her oversimplified understanding of the term—that she loves him. What is startling, however, is the way in which she seems to believe that her ease with him and various other "non-white" individuals somehow insulates her from any possibility of prejudice and bias. She does not "hate black people," I am fairly certain of this, but what is more chilling to me is the extent to which she lacks the mental bandwidth or desire to think very hard about experiences that differ even slightly from her own. Nothing about the way her life is set up forces or even incentivizes her to do it. This is the greatest obstacle to mutual understanding on a mass scale—and it is not a strictly white problem by any means.

I think often of a passage from Ta-Nehisi Coates's enormously successful and influential epistolary memoir *Between the World and Me*, in which he recounts an episode when an irritable white woman leaving an Upper West Side cinema pushes his young, "dawdling" [son] and impatiently screams, "Come on!" Coates, who is an imposingly built man, responds as follows:

> There was the reaction of any parent when a stranger lays a hand on the body of his or her child. And there was my own insecurity in my ability to protect your black body ... I was only aware that someone had invoked their right over the body of my son. I turned and spoke to this woman, *and my words were hot with all of the moment and all of my history.* She shrunk back, shocked. A white man standing nearby spoke up in her defense. I experienced this as his attempt to rescue the damsel from the beast. He had made no such attempt on behalf of my son. And he was now sup-

ported by other white people in the assembling crowd. The man came closer. He grew louder. I pushed him away. He said: "I could have you arrested!" I did not care. I told him this, and the desire to do much more was hot in my throat. [Emphasis my own.]

As Coates represents her, this woman is not a morally fallible, autonomous subject with her own biography and neuroses, but a representative of larger, impersonal social forces. I don't discount the possibility that she was a through-and-through racist, but he never extends to her the benefit of the doubt that she may be something else, even something equally unflattering, such as a nasty, petty individual who would have been just as likely to shove aside a blond or Chinese child standing in front of her. He doesn't appreciate that his disproportionate reaction—"my words were hot with all of the moment and all of my history"— is an unqualified overreaction and would likely be interpreted as such by those "standing nearby" for reasons that have to do with his size and intensity more than anything. It doesn't seem to strike him that as long as black people can be so easily triggered and provoked—so long as such barely submerged ancestral pain hovers just beneath the surface— we'll never be free or equal.

Elsewhere in the book, Coates confesses that he didn't really know any white people when he was a child: he only saw them on television. That is an indictment of our country's entrenched segregation, but even as an adult, he still seems not to know white people very well: He tends to attribute to them greater power and satisfaction with their lives than most of them have. He writes that whites "think that they are beyond the design flaws of humanity," although the profits of the pharmaceutical or self-help industries should be a red flag. When he visits Paris, he sees cartoon figures: "the men in salmon-colored pants and white linen and bright sweaters tied around their necks, the men who disappeared around corners and circled back in luxury cars, with the top down, loving their lives. All of them smoking. All of them knowing that either grisly death or an orgy awaited them just around the corner."

This is nonsensical, a fantasy that flattens psychological and material difference within and between groups, and only serves to bolster a permanent sense of injury that doesn't necessarily align with his own circumstance. If *this* is the means by which our nation's leading and most listened to public thinker and explainer of complicated matters of race and identity understands the actions, experiences, and motives of the various white people he encounters—with more force and eloquence than my cousin, no doubt, but with startlingly similar inflexibility and lack of generosity— then I fear we are going to be spending quite a lot of time talking past each other instead of reaching a common truth.

It was only in profiling and spending time with Adrian Piper in the spring of 2018 that I came to fully appreciate this tragic conundrum of racial incommunicability. In her 1992 essay "Passing for White, Passing for Black"—a bracingly candid look at how both blacks and whites misread and inadequately present themselves and misrepresent each other—Piper recounts experiences of having been mistaken for "white" by working-class blacks in Harlem who either teased her or required her to submit to a "Suffering Test." She notes that these exchanges were personally humiliating but useful in providing "insight into the way whites feel when they are made the circumstantial target of blacks' justified and deep-seated anger. Because the anger is justified and sometimes arbitrary, one's sense of fairness is violated. One feels both unjustly accused or harassed, and also remorseful and ashamed at having been the sort of person who could have provoked the accusation."

While in no way excusing anti-black racism, Piper nevertheless hits upon—a quarter of a century ago—a means of understanding (at least in part) the tortuous psychology of white reaction. A means that is rooted in an unusual dual perspective that feels far more useful in this era of rising populism than the one-size-fits-all contemporary discourse around implacable white supremacy that writers like Coates rely on. In such a situation as described above, Piper elaborates, "One can react defensively and angrily, and distill the encounter into slow-burning fuel for one's racist stereotypes. Or one can detach oneself emotionally and distance oneself physically from the aggressors, from the perspective of which their personal flaws and failures of vision, insight and sensitivity loom larger, making it easier to forgive them for their human imperfections but harder to relate to them as equals."

There are many racists, and we know this. In addition to the outright bigots, there are also many lazy white people like my cousin who may never be able to think hard enough about their own blind spots to become good-faith partners in any transformational exchange. But it is this last point of Piper's, this detached response she identifies—the distancing, and the concomitant and often subconscious condescension—that many whites who *could be* reached and who do not wish to think of themselves as racist nonetheless experience. This is some of what I so inadequately tried to convey to the troubled student who asked me why white people hate us. I try to keep Piper's insight in my mind even as I watch my relationship with members of my mother's family—to whom I find myself condescending—crumble, perhaps irrevocably, because of precisely this kind of fatal miscommunication.

I want to break the tortuous cycle, but the social media agora makes it continually more challenging. It has been several years now since Facebook revealed to me the deep conservatism of these family members on my mother's side. These are people, like my cousin Hope, that I have known and enjoyed in real life, mostly from a distance, but did not have an inkling of politically until we discovered each other on the social network at the end of the era of George W. Bush. Once we began to see each other virtually—and paradoxically both more fully and far more narrowly than ever before—we learned to navigate some awkward silences. But those videotaped extrajudicial police killings proved too much for our social media manners. My aunt's husband, a white veteran from rural Georgia, a man who had always been kind to me, began to refer to black people expressing anguish in such situations as "playing the race card," which alarmed me. A Bush voter, at one point he called the Obama administration a complete and total disaster, referring to the president as "the least intelligent" ever. It was a strange sensation for me to encounter my uncle like this, because while I know that he, too, would say he loves the non-white members of his family, these were sentiments clearly hardened by many years of racial calluses.

My uncle's and cousin's comments evoked in my mind a widely circulated and apocryphal tweet from a Chris Rock parody account after the Ferguson verdict: "Just found a new app that tells you which one of your friends are racist. It's called Facebook." Whatever ideological transparency that website may have fostered became unbearable in the run-up to and aftermath of the 2016 election. And this is a large part of what makes Coates's—and others'—uncompromising pessimism so compelling even as it remains so terribly self-defeating. I can't help but return to a feeling that has wracked me since the end of Obama's first term, after that rapturous and, in retrospect, impossibly short-lived promise of post-raciality began to fade in earnest: this disastrous backlash was—not completely but in some not-insignificant measure—a collective spasm of whatever sentiment it was my cousin and uncle had been voicing.

My own life has shown me repeatedly that racism at once persists and is also capable of being transcended— especially at the interpersonal level. With so many voices now directing generations of pent-up anger at targets that may not be wholly blameless but are at the same time too broad and categorical to entirely merit it—and with other voices both reacting to and exploiting this anger—how can we focus on the possibility of transcendence without being bogged down in recognition of the persistence of prejudice? When I was living in Berlin in the fall of

2017, I began to think a lot about the notion of *sonderweg* in the study of German history—literally the "special path" down which the German people have been fated to wander. In different eras, and depending on who employed it, the term could imply different things. It began as a positive myth during the imperial period that some German scholars told themselves about their political system and culture. During and after the Second World War it turned distinctly negative, a way for outsiders to make sense of the singularity of Germany's crimes. Yet whether viewed from within or without, left or right, the Germans could be seen through such a lens to possess some collective essence— a specialness—capable of explaining *everything* about them. In this way, one could speak of a trajectory "from Luther to Hitler" and interpret history not as some chaotic jumble but as a crisp, linear process.

There is something both terrifying and oddly soothing in such a formulation. For better or worse, it leaves many very important matters beyond the scope of choice or action. It imagines Germans as having been either glorious or terrible puppets, the powerful agents of forces nonetheless beyond their control. A similar unifying theory has been taking hold in America. Its roots lie in the national triple sin of slavery, land theft, and genocide. In this view, the conditions at the core of the country's founding don't just reverberate through the ages—they determine the present. No matter what we might hope, that original sin—white supremacy—explains everything, an all-American *sonderweg*.

The most shocking aspect of today's mainstream antiracist discourse is the extent to which it mirrors ideas of race—specifically the specialness of whiteness—that white supremacist thinkers cherish. "Woke" anti-racism proceeds from the premise that race is *real*—if not biological, then socially constructed and therefore equally if not more significant still—putting it in sync with toxic presumptions of white supremacism that would also like to insist on the fundamentality of racial difference. Working toward opposing conclusions, racists and many anti-racists alike eagerly reduce people to abstract color categories, all the while feeding off of and legitimizing each other, while any of us searching for gray areas and common ground get devoured twice. Both sides mystify racial identity, interpreting it as something fixed and determinative, and almost supernatural in scope. This way of thinking about human difference is seductive for many reasons but it has failed us.

In the years since the outcome of the 2016 election, I've been dismayed to see an opportunistic demagogue provoke racial resentment across the country and within families as well, but I've also been troubled to watch well-meaning white friends in my Twitter timeline and Facebook news feed flagellate themselves, sincerely or performatively apologizing for their "whiteness," as if they were somehow born into original sin. The writer and linguist John McWhorter (who happens to be black) has called this development "the flawed new religion" of Anti-racism, or "The current idea that the enlightened white person is to, I assume regularly (ritually?), 'acknowledge' that they possess White Privilege," he writes in a 2015 essay of the same name. "Classes, seminars, teach-ins are devoted to making whites understand the need for this. Nominally, this acknowledgment of White

Privilege is couched as a prelude to activism, but in practice, the acknowledgment itself is treated as the main meal ... The call for people to soberly 'acknowledge' their White Privilege as a self-standing, totemic act is based on the same justification as acknowledging one's fundamental sinfulness is as a Christian. One is born marked by original sin; to be white is to be born with the stain of unearned privilege." In other words, it is to walk that special path.

Without excusing the racists (or sexists) who by all indications are both numerous and emboldened, today's dominant liberal discourse—which sets up *all* whites as the nation's only genuine actors, and blacks and other minorities as their hapless props—has too often been counterproductive. George Packer, writing prophetically in the *New Yorker* about the populist tide that was swamping Hillary Clinton, spoke with the economist Glenn Loury (who also happens to be black) about the pyrrhic dimension of any identity politics victory. It's worth quoting at length. "As he sees it," Packer wrote of Loury, "if race becomes an irreducible category in politics, rather than being incorporated into universal claims of justice, it's a weapon that can be picked up and used by anyone. 'Better watch out,' [Loury] said. 'I don't know how you live by the identity-politics sword and don't die by it.' Its logic lumps everyone—including soon-to-be-minority whites—into an interest group. One person's nationalism intensifies tribal feelings in others, in what feels like a zero-sum game. 'I really don't know how you ask white people *not* to be white in the world we're creating,' Loury said. 'How are there not white interests in a world where there are these other interests?' He continued, 'My answer is that we not lose sight of the goal of racially transcendent humanism being the American bedrock. It's the abandonment of this goal that I'm objecting to.'"

Of course, black and other non-white people cannot meaningfully renounce their "race" if significant numbers of whites don't join them; but neither can even the best-intentioned white people do this in a vacuum. We are a composite nation as well as a nation of composites, and—alt-right fantasies of an all-white ethnostate in Montana and the Pacific Northwest notwithstanding*—we are stuck together. The racial resentments conjured and magnified by the 2016 election amount to a giant step in the wrong direction; it is impossible to deny that. But falling back into our narrow identities—even those forged by legitimate grievance and foisted upon us by the bigotry of others—only delivers a further victory to the opponents of a healthy society. To shift this dismal paradigm, thinking people of goodwill across the political spectrum are going to have to find a new vocabulary to move beyond abstract racial categorization and reflexive tribalism. Merely declaring race a construct won't be enough. "Treating race as a social fact amounts to nothing more than acknowledging that we were mistaken to think of it as a biological fact and then insist-

---

* The Northwest Territorial Imperative (or Northwest Imperative) is a white separatist dream popularized since the 1980s within white nationalist and white supremacist groups in the U.S. Like-minded whites are encouraged to relocate to a five-state swath of the Northwestern United States comprised of Washington, Oregon, Idaho, Wyoming, and Western Montana. (Northern California, Northwestern Colorado, Northern Utah, Alaska, British Columbia, and Alberta are sometimes also included.) The intent is to eventually declare the region an "Aryan" homeland.

ing that we ought to keep making the mistake," the literary theorist Walter Benn Michaels incisively points out in his book *The Trouble with Diversity*. A more durable rejection of Trumpism and the racism and xenophobia that animates it requires an appeal to deeper and more profound ways of not merely tolerating but integrating with each other. This in turn will have to be based on the convincing expression of shared ideals and democratic values that are accessible to all, regardless of personal background.

PAPPY VIGILANTLY REARED ME to brace myself for the challenges of being *seen* as a black man in America—for the various yokes, both visible and hidden, that act upon, in today's parlance, "black-looking bodies" and therefore an awful lot of black-feeling psyches. But even in the worst situations, these have hardly ever been more than vicariously mine. To my knowledge, in my adult life, I've never been harmed by my appearance or lineage, people don't cross the street when I approach, and the sole instance I've ever been pulled over in a car, I was speeding and I'll leave it at that. It's not that I've never experienced, or suspected I was experiencing, discrimination. And the situation doesn't have to be life-threatening or necessarily even violent to register as deeply jarring. There was that time years ago in Munich, when I was pointedly not allowed inside that same nightclub my blond friend Kevin was made to feel more than welcome to enter. Or the time in Manhattan when Josh and I went together into a business meeting and the white interlocutor could only bring himself to regard and address my

Jewish partner, even when responding to me. There have been other times in addition to these, however few and far between, in America and abroad. By orders of magnitude, I can fathom what it would mean to endure such slights daily and the doubt and sensitivity that would engender. Although there has been some ambiguity attached to my own nonwhite body, what I am most certain about in all of this—and at first it provided a source of paradoxical anxiety for me—is that there will not be with regard to my daughter's. She will not be turned away from that door or others just like it. And so as she grows and looks at me and smiles, all the while remaining innocent of all of this, I am left with a question: What of my people, whoever they may be, and of *me*, whoever I may be, is preserved in Marlow? And is whatever surface aspect that's been altered, in fact, the thing that's most important?

On this point, the preponderance of contemporary commentators on the subject, who cloak so much of the messiness and contradiction of lived experience in the false clarity of prefabricated rhetoric and the ethics of ressentiment, do not have answers for me. Virtually all of our most audible voices on race, today more than ever, in establishing identity solely in "the body"—no matter in how positive, persuasive, or righteously indignant a light—actually reinforce the same racist habits of thought they claim to wish to defeat. I do not mean this last point rhetorically—I mean it literally. Black Lives Matter, for example, is a cause whose aims—primarily the work of drawing attention to the severe abuses of the criminal justice system—I overwhelmingly share. Yet its very framing—the notion that some lives are *essentially* black while others are white—is both politically true in a specific sense and, in a broader way, philosophically inadequate. My cousin in California misses something crucial when she insists on an infantile colorblindness that allows her to escape the task of having to contemplate the possibility and pervasiveness of real injustice. But I am convinced that we will never be able to outwit such complicated and tenacious pathologies with the stale and deficient mental habits that produced them in the first place. If, as the cliché has it, one definition of insanity is doing the same thing over and over again but expecting different results, how could we?

A radical rethinking of "how racial differences are seen, how they appear to us and prompt specific identities," to quote Paul Gilroy again, is what is needed today. This means that we really do have to take seriously Frantz Fanon's appeal for a "new man" and then meet the task of inspiring him with life, sincerely, as a way of facing the world and making it our own. This is, without doubt, daunting even to contemplate. For my own part, I struggle to slough the feeling that I've arrived at an existential bind, in many ways similar to the one that grips secular Jews. The purpose of all these generations of struggle, I know, has always been the freedom to choose and create the self with dignity—but it is precisely this coveted self-regard and autonomy that threatens now to annihilate the very "racial" identity that won it in the first place. And yet that is precisely what has to occur—on a national scale. If we are ever to progress, we must first slough off these old skins we've been forced to don.

———

I UNDERSTAND THAT it is easier to entertain the kind of argument I would like to make, the more ambiguous your racial identity appears. Racism rooted in centuries of skin bias is persistent and feels more urgent than just about anything else when you bear the brunt of it. It can make other conversations seem luxurious if not irrelevant. But the situation is not zero-sum: We can simultaneously resist bigotry *and* imagine a society that has outgrown the identities it preys on. In fact, we have to. When I first delivered a lecture on the subject of this book (complete with photographic projections of my multihued family) while a fellow at the American Academy in Berlin in the fall of 2017, white American and German reactions to my talk seemed to run the gamut from vague incomprehension to polite if superficial support to a very enthusiastic desire for something like a genuine postracial future. (There may have also been outright condescension or disagreement, but I was not privy to it.) On the other hand, though multiple black attendees also expressed what seemed like heartfelt support for my position, others vocally did not. One colleague, B., a kind and thoughtful younger American academic, who is black, married to a white man, and had been raised in Zurich, challenged me during the question-and-answer period. I didn't know exactly how to respond: I disagreed on an intellectual level with her interpretation of my argument, but viscerally I felt something close to *repentant* for raising inconvenient objections to the racial status quo in front of her—objections to a status quo that was clearly not of her making or choosing but which had nonetheless so clearly upset her. A few days later, she expanded on what had so bothered her about my talk by email. These objections stayed with me because they conveyed in very thoughtful and compelling language much of the resistance that I have heard over and over again since I first began to question out loud my own continued allegiance to the color categories buttressing the American caste system. B.'s own work is geared toward excavating the long and fascinating history of black American involvement in European classical music, exploding the myth of racial categorization from the field of musicology. I find that her scholarship brilliantly undermines the subtle and not-so-subtle ways that people think of behaviors as essences. I would only add that it cannot stop there: if our behaviors are so demonstrably changeable, the truth is there is nothing much essential left.

One dilemma any argument against race must at some point contend with presents itself as the tension between universalism and particularism. B. expressed concern that appeals to universal values have really been a stand-in for white supremacy all along and, as such, another weapon turned on the oppressed, whose particularity (their blackness, or Hinduness) was forever a means of disqualification from the good life. Seen this way, the universal and the particular just function as two sides of the same coin of domination. People exalt the former not to reach *objective* truth—the "racially transcendent humanism" that is "the American bedrock," in Loury's words—but merely to assert and then exploit inevitable difference. And so white claims to liberty and equality brought about black slavery just as Enlightenment rationalism can be shown to have provided

Europeans with the intellectual, cultural, technological, and even moral basis for colonialism.

But these values—specifically, for my purposes, shared truth and equal worth—are like kilograms or Greenwich Mean Time: they don't exist by themselves; they always depend on real living people to be implemented. It is true that, historically, white freedom often depended on black (and to varying extents other forms of) unfreedom. Yet it doesn't follow that it must always be this way going forward. Until very recently, the institution of marriage between men and women was intimately bound to non-heterosexual couples' inability to be married. Cultures and societies, ways of seeing and ultimately ways of being, as well, can and do change when enough individuals open themselves up to that possibility. We've been thrust into a "world profoundly fissured by nationality, ethnicity, race, class, and gender," the scholar Henry Louis Gates, Jr., who happens to be black, has written. "And the only way to transcend those divisions—to forge, for once, a civic culture that respects both differences and commonalities—is through education that seeks to comprehend the diversity of human culture."

In other words, it is not incumbent to erase the particular or whitewash difference in order to recognize the possibility of, and aspire to, the universal. "Any human being sufficiently curious and motivated can fully possess another culture, no matter how 'alien' it may appear to be," Gates concludes. Which is simply to say, any human being properly motivated and educated is capable of outgrowing the bounds and divisions of identity, of touching the universal. If this is the case, and I have to believe it is, then the best aspects of

Enlightenment universalism—the belief in and search for unifying truth, and the power to discern it through reason tempered by tolerance for diverging opinions and views— can and should be salvaged and disentangled from the documented imperfections and biases of the past.

I say I have to *believe* it is possible that all human beings are capable of such transcendence. It's true this requires something along the lines of a leap of faith. I can't prove it mathematically. And so B. questioned to what extent any given individual can really be said to exercise agency. Her point being that if everything is absolutely determined by social structures, are people really able to assert or disavow their individual identities and personalities? Is it possible for a "black" person to reject being black once incoporated into a racialized society? The scholar Gayatri Spivak had recently visited the academy, and B. pointed out that for Spivak it is very difficult for the genuinely marginalized, or "subaltern," people even to *speak* against the societies in which they find themselves.

The conversation around determinism is tricky.* I'm not denying the practical impossibility of transcendence for my enslaved ancestors or even for Spivak's contemporary subaltern.† But I am talking about men and women

---

* To take it in another direction entirely, in his 2003 paper "Are You Living in a Simulation?" the Oxford philosopher Nick Bostrom popularized the simulation hypothesis, which holds that members of an advanced "posthuman" civilization with vast computing power might choose to run simulations of their ancestors in the universe. If this is possible, Bostrom argues, then it is almost inevitable. As such, the number of simulated universes would have to exponentially outnumber the one true "base reality," with the overwhelming odds being that ours is not the latter. So there's that.

† Though history does provide examples of slaves, from Epictetus to Frederick Douglass, who were capable of the most transcendent humanity. And Spivak

living in twenty-first century Western democracies being free enough to decide not to passively—or even just uncritically—reproduce their received racial designations. I know it's not fashionable today to call yourself an existentialist, but that is what I am, to the extent that I start from the premise that, though forces beyond my control influence and pressure and certainly constrict me, I am ultimately responsible for my own beliefs and actions. Even as a member of a historically oppressed minority, I can still define myself and in so doing exercise my agency, irrespective of how my society reacts to me.* Heidegger wrote of *thrownness*, the arbitrary aspect underpinning all of our lives, regardless of color or culture. We are all connected to a chain of past actions and social relations at once unchosen but in his view also not entirely deterministic of the future. I find this a most convincing description, though I realize it is ultimately speculative. One either accepts that human beings are subjects—something much more than pure reproductions of prefabricated

---

herself, in designating the subaltern, is painstakingly restrictive: "*Subaltern* is not just a classy word for 'oppressed,' for [the] Other, for somebody who's not getting a piece of the pie. . . . In post-colonial terms, everything that has limited or no access to the cultural imperialism is subaltern—a space of difference. Now, who would say that's just the oppressed? The working class is oppressed. It's not subaltern. . . . Many people want to claim subalternity. They are the least interesting and the most dangerous. I mean, just by being a discriminated-against minority on the university campus; they don't need the word 'subaltern.' . . . They should see what the mechanics of the discrimination are. They're within the hegemonic discourse, wanting a piece of the pie, and not being allowed, so let them speak, use the hegemonic discourse. They should not call themselves subaltern." From Leon de Kock, "Interview with Gayatri Chakravorty Spivak: New Nation Writers Conference in South Africa."

* *Within limits*—I am not saying that I can step outside tomorrow and declare myself a squirrel.

social structures—or one does not. But the fact remains that we all behave as though we act freely.

"I'd like to suggest that everyone who deliberates believes in free will, even if they think they do not," the philosopher and theologian Greg Boyd argues, "for it's impossible to deliberate without acting on the conviction that the decision is *up to you* to resolve." Just by arranging her argument about the dubiousness of human agency, B. has nonetheless exercised her own, weighing the merits and flaws of my lecture and choosing which points to include or exclude in her response to it. "People may sincerely *think* they believe in determinism, but they act otherwise, and must act otherwise, every time they deliberate," Boyd concludes. "The great American philosopher Charles Peirce argued that a belief that cannot be consistently acted on cannot be true." I have to accept a degree of agency in life because I know that I can't consistently put into practice the belief that I do not choose.

B. ALSO WONDERED whether I had paid sufficient attention to the field of critical mixed-race studies. It's not a frivolous point. There's a pervasive sense in the university—which amounts to a kind of territorialism—that one cannot engage a certain subject without first submitting to the conventions and dictates of whatever hyper-specialized subfield already regulates it. I am not an academic, and I don't subscribe to this view, but B. is right, other people have thought about these issues before me, and I have read much of what they have thought. (I have also weighed their ideas against my own experiences and observations.)

Scholarship on mixed and multiracial identity reaches back over a century, but the academic field of critical mixed-race studies, according to the *Journal of Critical Mixed Race Studies*, dates back only to about 2004. In a text from that journal entitled "Emerging Paradigms in Critical Mixed Race Studies," the authors G. Reginald Daniel, Laura Kina, Wei Ming Dariotis, and Camilla Fojas explain the discipline as bringing "into sharp focus the extensive 'racial blending' that has characterized human history from time immemorial but that has been ignored, obscured, and erased by several hundred years of Eurocentric thought supporting notions of racial (and cultural) purity." If in the past there has been a lack of "attention to the topic of multiracial identity," these scholars argue, it is "due in part to the fact that US social scientists, like the individuals and communities that were the primary focus of their studies, have internalized not only hypodescent [or, the one-drop rule] but also monoracial norms." CMRS then exposes the "mutability of race and the porosity of racial boundaries and categories" as it "interrogates racial essentialism and racial hierarchy."

This is vital work. Where I would vehemently differ with the CMRS movement and its authority over the subject is in the following statement of purpose from the same journal: "An interrogation of monoracial norms . . . should not be understood as a dismissal of monoracial forms of identification as illegitimate." Though I start from many of the same premises and observations, I want to end up at a much simpler and more definitive conclusion: If the idea of separate human races is a mistake to begin with, then monoracial forms of identification are fictitious and counterproductive. But so are stand-alone "mixed-race" identities, since everyone is in some way mixed to begin with.

Overlooking monoracial forms of identification is unlikely in practice, B. cautioned, because human physical variation—the kind that stirred Linnaeus to sort us in the first place—really is perceptible. She mentioned that unlike me or even herself, her brother is very dark. What would it look like for him to participate in this freedom? How, in other words, in rejecting race can we ever really escape the trap of colorism? Earlier, I mentioned Kmele Foster—a dark-skinned man who refuses to label himself as "black"— as an instance of admirable courage in the face of all the world's pressure to conform. I realize that his is likely too abrupt an abdication for most people to be able to emulate all at once.

There is also the incrementalism advised by Adrian Piper, who explained to me that anyone who is sufficiently motivated can reject their "race" first by thoroughly researching their own genetic and genealogical background and noting the variegated origins practically guaranteed to be found there.* From that point of departure, they might take the imperfect next step of describing themselves, when asked, as "mixed" instead of "black" (or "white"). This is not a final destination—the mistake I see in the field of critical

---

* For example, despite all appearances to the contrary, Foster traces Scottish ancestry in his background.

mixed-race studies—but a useful way station along the road to a full-scale rejection.

For someone like B.'s brother—whose physical appearance, like Kmele's but unlike Piper's, would likely cause other people, white and black alike, to disagree, possibly impolitely—participating in the kind of freedom I am talking about would look a lot like a rigorous intellectual or political project. It would amount to an achieved perspective that would require some real time and effort on his part to research and learn to articulate (just as it would for someone whose skin tone is a marker of "whiteness"). My honest expectation would be that, for him, participating in this freedom could very well entail getting laughed at. Not everyone can tolerate such derision, but certainly many more people who are convinced that there is something terribly inadequate about our current racial discourse and its implied hierarchy could look for ways to defy it. In so doing they would further lower the barrier of mockery for the next person. At various points in my own life, I have been laughed at scathingly for calling myself "black."* More recently I have been berated for rejecting the label. Both reactions are less than comfortable, but such discomfort may simply be, for now and the foreseeable future, the occasional levy placed against the act of self-definition. I think it is more than worth it.

Be that as it may, colorism is really just another way of speaking about power imbalances, B. pointed out, sounding

---

* Mostly this happened in high school, a status-stripping tactic used by certain black males in instances of conflict in which "blackness" is understood by all to denote virility and "whiteness" something more effete.

very much like my father.* Whether or not race exists, racism does, as does racial inequality. So where does that leave us? The work that most impacted my thinking on this point is a magnificent book from 2012 titled *Racecraft: The Soul of Inequality in American Life*, by Barbara and Karen Fields (a historian and sociologist respectively who refer to themselves as "Afro-American"). In it, the Fields sisters argue that racism creates race,† and not the other way around, while noting that despite our willingness as a society to speak out against racism, we nonetheless take the concept of race as an implacable given, and in so doing only perpetuate the problem. In coining the term "racecraft," they draw an analogy between the existence of human races and the existence of spirits and witches. Witches do not exist, they point out, but in many societies from colonial America to pre-Enlightenment Europe to parts of present-day Africa, real flesh-and-blood human women have been tried and killed for being just that. "In America, it is neither here nor there to affirm the truth that there are no races," the sisters write.

An even simpler analogy for race might just be currency: since we have left the gold standard, we all accept

---

* Indeed, this was his sole rationale for perpetuating the logic of the one-drop rule and raising my brother and me to believe in our "blackness" even while denying the existence of race. My father's view is that "might makes right" for most if not all intents and purposes, and that the hard reality is that anyone not deemed to be "white" in American society will be—to varying degrees based on many factors including color and sheer luck—fundamentally disempowered.

† For example—and leaving aside the issue of blackness—although distinct physical features are held to justify belief in separate races, the Irish and Jews are two peoples in American and European history that have been held apart from "whites" despite in many cases the impossibility of physically distinguishing them.

on one level that money is nothing but an abstraction, yet who would deny that the consequences of our collective credence in it are as real as gravity or cancer? If race is like money, then whiteness has been seen as the crispest hundred-dollar bill. The people who define themselves and are presently understood to be "white"—and this is an expansive and hodgepodge group of Americans who have changed and expanded over consecutive generations of immigration and miscegenation—tend to hold the most valuable form of social currency and benefit in real terms from all of our continued reliance on the idea of race. We can call this power arrangement white supremacy or white privilege or anything else we want, and lighter-skinned blacks and other non-black minorities may find ways to participate in it, too, because life is as bizarre as it is complex and contradictory. All of this is obvious. How is it any less clear that acknowledging this state of affairs should provoke as many blacks, Asians, Latinos, and whites of goodwill as possible to voluntarily remove themselves from the confidence game? At the very least, it should leave all those deemed "non-white" with scant incentive to continue reinvesting in such a bankrupt farce.

In practice, any real and widespread disinvestment from the politics of racial identity—and resentment—would almost necessarily have to coincide with a reawakening of consciousness of class. Faced as we are with enormous societal challenges that cut across racial lines, this would be a most positive development. Entire *classes* of Americans who are in fact all more or less vulnerable to everything from militarized police* to the unavailability of affordable medicine to the reality of rising shorelines will have to find the language and imagination to create common cause. (The mobilization around Bernie Sanders's 2016 presidential campaign provided one unexpectedly persuasive glimpse of what this might look like.)

And yet I am aware that the reality is more complicated than that. There is, for example, the fact of great diversity within the black experience. The removal of race, B. warned, though on its face a potential good, could nonetheless amount to a larger erasure. Everyone accepts that race is not biologically grounded, she conceded, but how else are we to worship, make art, or narrate our lives? Culturally speaking, blackness has given us some extraordinary products, from the writings of Langston Hughes to the paintings of Romare Bearden to Michael Jackson's moonwalk. People *like* these things, as they should. How else would we organize ourselves in cultural terms if not along the contours of race?

One of the saddest things I've realized while researching and writing about this topic over the past several years is that *not* everyone agrees that race is merely a social construct—not by a long shot. In the summer of 2017, while reporting on the influence of French and German think-

---

* Despite prevailing media narratives, a militarized police presence is a threat to all Americans, not just blacks. According to "The Counted: People Killed by Police in the U.S.," a database maintained by the *Guardian*, 1,093 Americans were killed by police in 2016. Of that total, 574 were white, 266 were black, 183 were Latino, 24 were Native American, 21 were Asian/Pacific Islander, and 24 were other/unknown. The worst rate per million—by far—belonged to Native Americans, at 10.13. For blacks it was 6.66; for Latinos, 3.23; for whites, still the largest demographic, the figure was 2.9. Asian deaths, at 1.17, were very rare.

ers on the American alt-right, I interviewed the virulently racist white nationalist Richard Spencer. He made it clear that he and those white supremacists who think along similar lines want nothing less than to reinvigorate the idea of biological race in the hearts and minds of everyday white Americans. "I one hundred percent believe that race has a biological-physical component that is totally indispensable," he told me. As I have already noted, such thinking was indeed discredited in the liberal consensus following the Second World War. In the mainstream media and in academia we have, superficially at least, accepted that race is a social construct even if it is not a scientific reality. But on other social frequencies—which do not function along the conventions of a graduate seminar—Spencer reiterated something I have long suspected, which is that many white people privately sense *there is something genetic* about race. They simply have learned not to say so openly to avoid being labeled racist.

Perhaps more importantly, though, "groundbreaking advances in DNA sequencing technology have been made over the last two decades," the Harvard geneticist David Reich argued in a widely circulated 2018 op-ed in the *New York Times*. "These advances enable us to measure with exquisite accuracy what fraction of an individual's genetic ancestry traces back to, say, West Africa 500 years ago—before the mixing in the Americas of the West African and European gene pools that were almost completely isolated for the last 70,000 years. With the help of these tools, we are learning that while race may be a social construct, differences in genetic ancestry that happen to correlate to many of today's racial constructs are real."

Reich's point is not at all the same as Spencer's. His was a cautionary note. "If scientists can be confident of anything, it is that whatever we currently believe about the genetic nature of differences among populations is most likely wrong," he cautioned. I take that warning seriously and am prepared to accept that there can be differences between large and isolated genetic pools without turning these potential differences into more insidious and nebulous claims about racial essences.

"Compared with the enormous differences that exist among individuals, differences among populations are on average many times smaller, so it should be only a modest challenge to accommodate a reality in which the average genetic contributions to human traits differ," Reich concludes. Yet it is crucial "to face whatever science will reveal without prejudging the outcome and with the confidence that we can be mature enough to handle any findings. Arguing that no substantial differences among human populations are possible will only invite the racist misuse of genetics that we wish to avoid."

But what if I am overstating these points and everyone really does accept that race is cultural and not biological? Is this really such a good thing? If human beings are not members of scientifically measurable "bioraces," then why pretend as though they are? Why do the work of making race by other, non-scientific means? If witchcraft isn't real, then why pretend as though witches walk among us? When I asked Adrian Piper, the artist who "retired" from being black, whether she believed there was even something so straightforward as a "black" sensibility, she denied it. Her point, which is worth taking seriously, is similar to Henry Louis Gates, Jr.'s: All human culture is available and knowable to all human beings. (Which is not quite the same as saying all human culture is equally important to all human beings.)

What is a black sensibility, then? What, even, is a black culture? There are the tastes, traditions, values, achievements, aversions, beliefs, superstitions, and, yes, even the *genes*—the circumstances—of specific groups of people at specific periods of time. We may feel close to these and cherish and preserve them, even feel personally defined by them. Yet within those many different confines, human life still remains far too surprising to end up with sweeping statements that can hold up in the face of scrutiny.

Many of those deemed "black" Americans have made enormous contributions to music and dance, an indisputable fact. Does that mean it is *inherently* part of "black" culture to dance well,* as Piper herself does and has documented throughout her career in hypnotizing video performances? She would say, not so fast: There are "black" people who are lamentable dancers (such as myself) even as there are "white" and "Asian" men and women who dance with

---

* In his essay "Context and Choice in Ethnic Allegiance," the sociologist Orlando Patterson observes, for example, "What is important about the American Jews is not the fact that they worship on Saturdays, or that they have certain unique rituals or patterns of socialization, but the functions of these rituals for the group—the ways in which they are used to maintain group cohesiveness, sustain and enhance identity, and to establish social networks and communicative patterns that are important for the group's optimization of its socioeconomic position in the society. A theory of ethnic cultural elements and symbols is an absurdity, because these symbols are purely arbitrary and unique to each case." In other words, it could always be *otherwise*.

extraordinary rhythm and grace in any style you can conceive of, from the *pas de deux* to the Milly Rock. Dancing itself is beside the point. What matters is the meaning certain groups have chosen over time to attach to it.

This is not to say that "black" people didn't create jazz or the blues, and in so doing bring into the world magnificent cultural treasures. It's just that a distinct community of people in a given place and time, drawing on inherited habits and influences in new technological and social realities, accomplished these feats and in so doing initiated traditions that have been upheld largely but not at all exclusively by subsequent generations who resemble them. One does not need to alter one's appreciation of or relationship to these achievements or traditions in order to search for new ways of engaging, belonging to, and recognizing each other that are not invested with essentializing notions of identity, whether biological or socially construed. On the contrary, one can easily deny the abstract racial classification *and* embrace the real communities and cultural traditions inspired by it. My father didn't often listen to the stereo, but when he did, it was almost always to play a James Brown record. I love the sound of this music, and to this day when I put on "The Payback," it aligns me with a tradition that is larger than either of us and makes me emotional. The connection is paternal, communal, and deeply meaningful, yet it need not be mystified as racial.

I AM AWARE—and from time to time still feel it in myself—of the terror involved in imagining a total absence of race. And I'm also aware that this conversation with B. has remained somewhat theoretical. At the end of her message, she brought the conversation to a far more specific and personal note that really touched me, writing of the decades-long struggle she endured just to accept her own body as a brown-skinned, curly-haired girl growing up in Switzerland. She confessed to having, at times, wished to be white simply to make her life easier. What saved and empowered her was intensive study in the history of black classical musicians and leaders like Marian Anderson, W. E. B. Du Bois, and Mary Church Terrell. The discovery of Beyoncé helped, too. After all this time and effort to accept and repurpose the race that had been heaved on her by Western society, how can she now just stop being black?

What B. is really talking about here is *self-image*. The great writer Albert Murray, who passed in 2013, and whose 1970 masterpiece *The Omni-Americans* does more than just about any other text I am aware of to convey the three-dimensionality of *Homo Americanus*—"part Yankee ingenuity, part backwoodsman/Indian or gamecock of the wilderness, and part Negro"—argues that contemporary usage of descriptors like "black" and "white," drenched as they are in non-science, are unhelpful. For Murray, African-Americans (those people whose culture is "truly indigenous" to the United States) incorporate all the essential identities and experiences within themselves and exemplify the fundamentally "mongrel" nature of the land.

But he also believed that people live in terms of images and that the prevailing ones of black people (but the insight can apply to many other groups, as well) as consummate victims of white supremacy—regardless of who generates them—are inadequate. B. worked her way out of a harming idea of herself that was based in racist rejection, and found strength in the lives of others who were also designated black* but who refused to allow themselves to be defeated. In a most powerful sense, she shifted her set of images. I am only questioning why the identification must be understood strictly—or even primarily—in terms that are held to be racial. These are men and women whose life circumstances and work can—and *do*—inspire all kinds of people, many of whom are not black. Likewise, black people can be—and *are*—inspired by everyone from Shakespeare to the Buddha. We don't have to limit our points of reference and inspiration to identity groups that perpetuate the idea of racial difference. We can also choose to expand our vision of ourselves, and bring about a fuller rendering of our common, complex human condition.

Just as a child does not automatically loathe her own body, neither does she automatically organize the world racially. These impulses must be learned through contact with others. Unlearning them happens the same way, and through serious and sustained self-reflection, both of which are really what saved B., not race-consciousness per se. It

---

* Beyoncé's own racial messaging has sometimes been nuanced. The stand-alone video for *Lemonade*'s first single "Formation" is a surreal, politically inflected amalgamation of images of Louisiana that evoke Hurricane Katrina. Transcendent, unsinkable Beyoncé perches atop a police cruiser and sings of herself: "My daddy Alabama, Momma Louisiana / You mix that Negro with that Creole make a Texas bama." This reference to her parents is not the only time Beyoncé has identified as something *other* than wholly black—she was once described as "African-American, Native American and French" in an advertisement for L'Oréal.

took me months of thinking about my own biases and limitations, of living with B.'s objections, especially this last part, which could be the objections of so many people I love and care about, before I found myself ready to respond to them. The process drove me back to Murray, for whom the cultural artifact that is most instructive is the blues—in the most extra-musical sense of the term. For Murray, the ingenious strength of this "equipment for living"—not just a genre but a form of stoic philosophy, artistry, and aesthetics developed and elaborated by tenacious slaves and their descendants—lay in its power to reconfigure the terms of the existential debate. Real dignity, as he saw it, the kind that can never be stripped from you because only *you* have the power to bestow it upon yourself, comes from accepting and playing the hand you are dealt as best you can. It also comes from understanding and accepting that no one else has a perfect hand, whatever the appearances.

What I would like to tell B. now is the same thing I intend to tell my children when they are older. It's the same thing I had to tell myself when, after thirty-three years of never questioning, with the shock of my daughter before me, I finally faced myself in the mirror and decided I could no longer allow the customs and images of the plantation— of the *slaver*—to be my own, no matter what good may have also been done through them. The intellectual and cultural discoveries that sustained us are ours forever. But the "dreadful deceit" that would call these things *racial* is just that, a lie that can never be made noble.

It is my hope that as many people as possible, of all skin tones and hair textures, will come to turn away from the

racial delusion. But I don't think it would be unfitting in
the least for blacks to take the lead here. Not only do we
have the most to gain from the dismantling of the American
white-black binary, we also have scarce incentive to wait for
all or even most of the people deemed white to get on board
with us. Everything B. acknowledges above goes to show
the way in which race—and the invented category of blackness in which she, like my father and like myself, has been
thrown—has functioned as a *problem* to solve in her life, dis-
tracting her from other pursuits, draining precious mental
and spiritual energy. That race was not created by the people
it most powerfully oppresses is an objection that resonates
emotionally, but once we accept that truth, it does little to
move us forward. The party at fault for a wrong is not necessarily the party best situated to address and heal it. The
writer Coleman Hughes, channeling the controversial legal
scholar Amy Wax's "Parable of the Pedestrian," from her
2009 book *Race, Wrongs, and Remedies*, illustrated this point
in a powerful if terribly challenging argument about intergenerational poverty in the black community. As a thought
experiment, it works equally well for our purposes:

> A reckless driver runs a stoplight and hits a pedes-
> trian, injuring her spine. Doctors inform the
> pedestrian that if she ever wants to walk again she'll
> have to spend many painstaking years in physical
> therapy. Clearly, she bears no responsibility for her
> injury; she was victimized by the reckless driver. Yet
> the driver cannot make her whole. He might pay for
> her medical bills for instance, but he cannot make her

attend her tedious physical therapy sessions; only she can do that. Still, she might resist. She might write historical accounts detailing precisely how and why the driver injured her. When her physical therapists demand more of her, she might accuse them of blaming the victim. She might wallow in the unfairness of it all. But this will change nothing. The nature of her injury precludes the possibility of anyone besides her healing it.

The nature of the vast and old—but not nearly eternal—racial injury visited upon all of us, because it does harm us all, but visited with special vehemence upon blacks as a group is inherently an injustice. Let us acknowledge this, let us grieve about it when we need to, but above all let us earnestly search for and find ways to fix it. I can think of no better start than rejecting the very logic that created and perpetuates the injury in the first place.

FOR ANYONE who is doubtful of the sheer absurdity of racial categorization and the porousness of our supposed boundaries, Adrian Piper's family history can be instructive. Adrian Margaret Smith Piper was born in 1948 in Washington Heights, and raised there and on Riverside Drive. On her paternal side, she is the product of a long line of whites and extremely light-skinned, straight-haired black property owners and, on her mother Olive's side, mixed-race, planter-class Jamaican immigrants. Her father, Daniel, received two separate and contradictory birth certificates.

The first one labeled him as "white," while the second, which his mother demanded as a corrective, put him down as "octoroon," or one-eighth black. Piper's paternal grandfather, also Daniel, went the opposite route after the birth of his second, slightly darker son, Billy, abandoning his wife and children and moving out West to start a new "white" family in Washington State. Daniel Sr.'s brother, Piper's great-uncle, William, lived his life as a Caucasian man of distinction, founding the Piper Aircraft Corporation and making his name as "the Henry Ford of Aviation." He ended up with his face on a postage stamp and a fortune big enough to endow an auditorium at his alma mater, Harvard.

Piper's father grew up more privileged than most Americans of any complexion, attending a private school in the city, where he was a handsome and popular athlete. But in his senior year, when he made the mistake of asking out a white classmate, he was publicly shamed and removed from the basketball team. In her memoir *Escape to Berlin*, Piper writes that the incident caused her father to suffer a psychological trauma of such severity that "he stopped speaking to all of his classmates and teachers for the rest of the year." While serving in the military during World War II, he strategically enlisted as Caucasian, concerned that he would not otherwise see combat. But the racism he became privy to as a "white" man appalled him, and he never again wavered from his black identity upon returning to civilian life.

What *is* race if a man, at various stages, can be *either* "black" or "white"? In my own family, when I look to my mother's side and I see my aunt Shirley's Facebook posts about our immigrant ancestors diligently pulling themselves up and out of Germany, or to my father's side on Ancestry.com and stare into the abyss of chattel slavery, I concur that race is hardly more than the difference between those who descend from the free and those who do not. But I am also aware that *I* have always been free and I am free right now—and I intend to stay that way. So why should I allow the slaver's perception to define *me*? Why should *you*?

It wasn't until I found myself having dinner with Piper at a restaurant situated in a former Jewish girls' school in East Berlin—well after I'd begun thinking and writing about my own family's "racial" shift—that it became clear to me that genuine liberty, inner, mental freedom, is never something another person can give to you but rather something hard-won that anyone interested will eventually have to take for herself, will have to seize with conviction, if she will have it at all. Since any child knows that as soon as you begin to define yourself on your own terms people will mock and scorn you, self-creation comes as the result of disregard for both of these mechanisms of conformity and control. Piper's retirement no longer seemed a mere art gesture or a statement of eccentricity to me that evening in Berlin, but the embodiment of Camus's injunction: her self-defined existence *was* an act of the most extreme rebellion in the face of racism—that raging global forest fire whose oxygen is first and foremost belief in the racial fiction.

The thing that had always made me hesitate, though, that had made me cleave to an interpretation of myself as "black"—even to linger in the masochistic grip, against all logic, of the one-drop rule—was the vaguest sense of indebtedness to past suffering. In other words it was a form of guilt, pure and simple. Other people who had come before me, people who had almost certainly suffered inexplicable pain and to whom I literally owed my life—at least in part—had been given the label "black" (or its derogatory precursors) and had found ways to triumph in spite of it. They had made something beautiful from it, too. The stories of their circumstances inspired me and still do. So I pledged allegiance to that label not because I thought it just or even accurate but simply because I wanted to honor the pain as well as the triumph. I did not want to forget it.

Piper and I had been talking for hours and these qualms, however faintly, lingered when I showed her the picture of Marlow that is the wallpaper on my iPhone. She's three years old there and standing on the edge of a jetty in Sweden, gazing across the rippling Baltic. Her skin is ivory, her eyes are a limpid blue like the water, and an ever-so-incongruent puff of golden curls levitates above her neckline. I often marvel that in the not-so-distant past, Marlow—like my father and me, though not like my wife or my mother—would have been enslaved by people who *looked just like her*. Piper smiled at the photo and listened as I tried to explain that it worried me that Marlow might not also *feel* guilty.

"Why would you want that in the first place?" she asked me matter-of-factly. "If the pain and the guilt isn't there, why introduce it?" The question, so simply put and so deceptively difficult to counter, surprised me. No one I had ever spoken to—and especially no one who was black, or Jewish, for that matter—had ever rejected the premise of allegiance to pain on its face. But why not? It seemed of a piece with something Richard Wright once stated: Every hour that a man is fighting for his freedom is an hour that he is not free.

I sat there and stared at my plate and finally told Piper that I thought she was right, and that, emboldened in no small part by her example, I, too, was retiring from race, so to speak—stepping out of that flawed and cruel game. As we said goodbye and I left the restaurant and walked back to my hotel room, I realized that nothing had changed, nothing that was inside me or fundamental to my self-conception. My love for the culture of my family and my loyalties were intact. My values were, too. These would be the love, loyalties, and values I would transmit to my daughter. But I would not willfully pass on to her the guilt and the pain of an artificial and externally imposed identity the belief in which has been harming one half of my ancestors since the moment the first one stepped off the boat from Africa, even as it disfigured the other, European half who have allowed themselves to be defined against it.

And, though no one else in that unseasonably warm and bustling cobblestone street in Mitte could discern any transformation, I did understand that I was no longer the same as when I had entered the restaurant that evening. Silly as it may seem, Piper's mere act of questioning a premise I had not known could be questioned had unloosed something inside me. The title of this chapter, which had until then made only abstract sense to me—even as it felt wholly forbidden—now seemed like a foregone conclusion. I'd become an *ex-black* man on that evening, not because I'd ceased loving what I've been taught to call "black," or because I now wished my daughter to blend in to what I'd been taught to call "white," but simply because these categories cannot adequately capture either of us—or anyone else, for that matter. I had no guilt about it anymore because blackness, like whiteness, isn't real.

EPILOGUE

THE SHAPE OF THINGS
TO COME

USED TO HAVE A KIND OF RECURRING DAYDREAM SEVERAL years ago. It's a couple of decades into the future, and there's a young woman with pale skin and blond hair and light blue eyes. She's seated at a café table somewhere in Europe. And this young woman, perhaps she is gathered with work colleagues, offhandedly remarks—in the dispassionate tone of one of my old Catholic-school classmates claiming to have a dash of Cherokee or Iroquois blood—that as improbable as it may seem, she once had black ancestors in America. She says it all so matter-of-factly, with no visceral aspect to the telling. I imagine the vague surprise of the people she is sitting with, perhaps a raised eyebrow or two or perhaps not even that—and if I want to torture myself, I detect an ironic smirk or giggle. Then, to my horror, I see the conversation grow not ugly or embittered or anything like that but simply pass on, giving way to other, lesser matters, plans for the weekend or questions about the menu, perhaps. And then it's over. Just like that, in one casual exchange, I see a history, a struggle, a culture, the whole vibrant and populated world of my ancestors—and of myself—dissolve into the void. I see a potential Marlow that I could no longer recognize.

To this day, feelings something like panic still creep in. On the one hand, there is the acute and very specific panic of wondering if I have indeed, along with my brother, permanently altered the culture or mind-set or physiognomy or, yes, the very "*race*" of an entire line of people, like a freight train slowly but irrevocably switching tracks. On the other, there is the subtler, lower-decibel, gnawing panic, which manifests as a plain awareness of the unearned advantage. It is impossible not to feel that. At a time when, despite all of the tremendous societal progress, blackness—certainly not always but especially at that vexed intersection with poverty or the cultural signifiers of such—is still subject to all manner of violation and disrespect; at a time when people perceived as black continue to be stopped, frisked, stalked, harassed, choked-out, and drilled with bullets in broad daylight and left to bake in the street—what does it mean to have escaped a fate? Put baldly, what is proximity to the idea of whiteness worth and what does color cost? And the reverse?

These are questions I'm still learning how to answer. With the recent birth of my second child, Saul, a six-week-old Venetian blond, with even bluer eyes than his sister's, the questions have evolved to encompass subtler aspects of gender, too. I suspect it will be something else altogether to raise a white-looking male. But I have also learned to pose the questions in other ways now. I have begun to acknowledge—to myself mostly, but more and more when others ask—that what I have proximity to is, in fact, neither whiteness nor blackness in the abstract but actual family and friends, which is to say real flesh-and-blood people, of different hues and heritages, nothing more or less. "But any fool can see that the white people are not really white and that black people are not black." It is worth repeating Albert Murray's point, which I have begun to insist on, timidly at first but with growing confidence as the days of my new familial reality have accumulated out of mere conjecture and into the stuff of real life. I am determined to live with precisely this level of childlike foolishness. It is the only antidote I'm yet aware of to the poisonous disingenuousness of an adult world that deploys color metaphors to sort people into real-life castes—color castes capable of insidiously coopting even anti-racist resistance into further reinforcement of those same illegitimate and consequential terms.

About the dual plight of the anti-Communist dissident, Ryszard Kapuscinski wrote potently and in ways that speak to the subtle dangers those of us who would oppose racism face when opposing it while continuing to accept—even for the sake of argument—the dubious premise of race. "On this subject [the dissident] can discourse with energy and passion for hours," Kapuscinski writes, "concoct schemes, present proposals and plans, unaware that as he does so he becomes for a second time communism's victim: the first time he was a victim by force, imprisoned by the system, and now he has become a victim voluntarily, for he has allowed himself to be imprisoned in the web of communism's problems. For such is the demonic nature of great evil—that without our knowledge and consent, it manages to blind us and force us into its straitjacket." We could substitute the word "race" in the above passage at each instance of "communism" and arrive at a parallel insight about the nature of an even larger system of "great evil" that ensnares us all; it would perhaps become even more convincing in the process. The truth is that no matter how long and hard you try— you cannot struggle your way out of a straitjacket that does not exist. But pretending it exists, for whatever the reason, really does leave you in a severely restricted posture. I want to stand tall, with my full range of motion intact.

What I know now is that I used to not just tolerate but submit to and even on some deep level *need* our society's web of problems called race, its received and dangerous habits of thinking about and organizing people along a binary of white and black, free and unfree, even once I suspected them to be irredeemably flawed. Baldwin pointed out that it is so much easier to sink deeper into a lukewarm bath than to stand and walk away. He was correct, but for my children's sake if not my own, I can't linger any longer. Now, if I find liberation in moments of doubt, it comes with the one movement I always end up having to make, the only movement I *can* make—away from the abstract, general, and hypothetical and back into the jagged grain of the here and now, into the humanizing specificity of my love for my father, mother, brother, wife, and children, and into my sheer delight in their existence as distinct and irreplaceable people, not "bodies"—as contemporary lingo would have it—or avatars, sites of racial characteristics and traits, reincarnations of conflicts and prejudices past. Through these people I love, I am left with myself as the same, as a man and a human being who is free to choose and who has made choices and is not reducible to a set of historical circumstances and mistakes.

A few weeks after Saul was born, Valentine and I spent several weeks at an old rented house in the Luberon region of Provence. Over the course of our stay many different family members and friends came to meet the baby, swim, and pass the cool mornings and the starlit nights on the terrace overlooking a valley of vineyards and umbrella pines. Blacks (of a variety of mixes), Jews, gentiles, Arabs, Asians, French-speakers (some with roots in the former colonies, some with the prefix "de" in their family names), and plain-old Americans all passed through, all broke bread, all sipped the same wine. What was exceptional in this painfully tribal world was how normal and natural it all seemed. I don't know if I can ever attain—or should want to attain—a state where I do not notice the various ethnic and social differences among us, but I have already ceased to allow those differences to dominate and determine the exchange.

While at the house, most mornings I would strap Saul to my chest and pace the terrace to calm him while Valentine recouped some of the sleep she'd lost while nursing the night before. One day, I was rereading Camus as my footsteps lulled my son to sleep. The massif of the Luberon, the slash of mountain framing my view, would have been familiar to the great writer. After an impoverished childhood in Algeria and a meteoric rise in Paris, several years before he died in a horrific crash, Camus used his Nobel earnings to buy a home in the nearby medieval town of Lourmarin, where the simplest stone slab marks his grave in the sunniest cemetery I have ever seen. The elements and the years have nearly wiped away his name, but whenever we are in the area, we manage to find that stone and bow our heads. We had visited the grave the previous day, and as I was pacing with Saul, I shielded his nearly translucent skin from the blazing light with one hand and scrolled across a line from Camus on the phone I held in the one that was free. "Poverty kept me from thinking all was well under the sun and in history," he wrote. But "the sun taught me that history was not everything."

The loudest and most insistent voices dominating the conversation around race today are radically out of step with such a wise and supple view. All seem to have rigidly subscribed to William Faulkner's not completely mistaken insight (though Faulkner himself would certainly prove problematic today) that "the past is not dead, it's not even past." History is everywhere and all around us, these voices remind us as they pounce on past atrocities—many of which I've tried to explore in these pages—with an almost masochistic glee: the United States was founded on the triple sin of slavery, genocide, and theft of land. The majority of the world has been subjugated under the yoke of European colonialism. The poor everywhere are sacrificed at the altar of capitalist greed. The plague of white supremacy—spreading now through the United States and Europe—as Camus warned us never entirely goes away, it only lies dormant for a spell. All of this is *true*—in part at least, since reality is always stubbornly more complicated—yet the formulation that holds that we are merely beholden to uncountable deeds and decisions already concluded misses something of equal veracity that Camus understood well and that I felt I could see right then—could even feel it on my skin. History has many noble uses. I grasp the context in which it arrives, for example, that my father inherited less wealth from his people than my mother did from hers. And so I understand the policy implications and historical processes this expresses, and this awareness gives me both perspective as well as empathy and also humility when I think of what he went through in order, specifically, to right for his children some of these enormous collective wrongs. But history's utility, while necessary, is diminished greatly when it smothers the light of the present day, overshadowing the genuine possibility and beauty the here and now may contain with reference to nothing further than itself. We have a responsibility to remember, yes, but we also have the right and I believe even the duty to continuously remake ourselves anew.

There is a millennia-old philosophical experiment called Theseus's paradox or the ship of Theseus about the mythical founding-king of Athens who kept a thirty-oar vessel docked in the harbor. The ship was preserved in a seaworthy state through the continual replacement of old timber planks with new ones, piecemeal, until the question inevitably arose: After all of the original planks have been replaced by new and different planks, is it still, in fact, the *same* ship? I learned about the paradox in college but it acquired the power to haunt me around the same time I began to have that daydream about the girl from the future, sitting at her café table discussing the ironies of ancestry with her new and unknowable friends. *Will it or won't it be the same ship?* I once posed the question to an old childhood friend. We were sitting in my parents' backyard in New Jersey, Marlow was playing on the grass in the distance. My friend, who is "black" (though if he is on average, as I suspect, he is also significantly "mixed"), thought hard and replied that, for better or worse, he saw a different ship. Yet the question is a trap. The answer depends on what you see when you look at the vessel—do you believe that color is inherent (let alone meaningful), or are you willing to entertain that whatever color you might think you see is itself the result of the perceptive act?

Not a day passes that I do not try to imagine the person my daughter—and now my son along with her—will be shaped into, the places where she will feel at home, and the ways she will learn to perceive. And what I'd want to say to that future Marlow is this: The drive to flatten difference, the inclination to erase and define ourselves against some *other*, is something we can never allow ourselves to condone. We must always be on the side that celebrates and cultivates variety, accepting without fetishizing difference. We must confront our own biases at every turn. I would remind her of another age-old experiment: Take a chicken, hold its head to the ground, and draw a line with a stick; when you let go it will stay there, hypnotized and unable to move, though it is free as ever to take flight. What I'd explain to this future Marlow is that we are not chickens, and the past sketched all around us in fading marks cannot immobilize us unless we allow it to. I would want her to know that as long as she lives, there will be more and more people like her, people who are more than what at first they seem. What might all of our lives look like if they—and the rest of us who are willing along with them—decided to lift ourselves up and walk away?

ACKNOWLEDGMENTS

'D BEEN WORKING ON A NOVEL (PERHAPS IT WAS ILL-conceived; perhaps the conception was fine and I just didn't have the tools yet to execute it properly) for three years when my daughter, Marlow, was born, in October 2013. It seemed entirely plausible that it might take me another three years to find my footing. But her arrival shifted my focus, almost immediately. Soon, I realized I was writing an essay about some of the questions her appearance prompted in me. I put the novel aside and eventually published "Black and Blue and Blond" in *Virginia Quarterly Review* in winter 2015. It has taken me four more years to expand that essay into this book, and I am certain that I needed to grow and develop as a husband, son, brother, and father, let alone writer, in order to do it. This book is impossible, then, without Marlow and her little brother, Saul.

In addition to my children, I need to thank my wife, Valentine, for her almost limitless patience and curiosity, as well as unwavering support and, at times, very healthy skepticism in discussing the ideas in this book. I also need to thank her simply for allowing me to portray our family and hers with candor in the context of what is a very tricky subject. This is something that is not at all easy to do, and she never once attempted to censor a single word.

No matter how far away I get, "I am always going home, always to my father's house," as Novalis wrote. There are certain formative impressions, quandaries, and truths I realize now I will never outgrow. I have to thank my father and also my mother for giving me one of my lifelong subjects as well as my confidence, my education, and also my model for racial transcendence in both theory and practice. Big ups to my brother, Clarence, too, for riding this road with me.

Without the support, encouragement, and extremely helpful edits of Ralph Eubanks at VQR, I don't know that I would have gotten the original essay off the ground. I am also grateful to Jonathan Franzen for taking the time to read "Black and Blue and Blond" and including it in *The Best American Essays 2016*. That selection was a crucial shot in the arm while I was working on the proposal and questioning how to proceed.

Some proposals are harder to write than others, and this was not an easy one. I can't imagine a better, kinder, or more diligent agent than Adam Eaglin at Cheney Literary. He is an agent, but he is also a gifted editor, and we worked through dozens of drafts together, all of which were painful, and all of which made the book much stronger.

I need to thank John Glusman at Norton not only for believing in this project from the outset but also for fighting for it during a publishing season when some of the ideas certainly cut against consensus. John's patience, tact, and gentle encouragement when life's vicissitudes kept pushing my timeline back—not to mention his judicious edits—were what got this book finished.

I am deeply indebted to George Packer and Yascha Mounk, two extraordinarily generous and insightful early readers whose last-minute feedback allowed me to break through several lingering problems I could not see clearly on my own.

I want to thank all of the staff and community at the MacDowell Colony, The American Academy in Berlin, and New America. Support from these institutions has been life-changing, and the men and women working at them go so far beyond the call of duty, they become friends.

The journalism I was able to produce while working on this book has been extremely formative, and a number of ideas I tried out first in shorter pieces have found their way in here. Editors, copy editors, and fact-checkers make huge and selfless contributions to work someone else ultimately takes credit for. So, I need to thank in particular the wonderful editorial staffs at the *New York Times Magazine*, the *New York Times* op-ed page, the *American Scholar*, and the *London Review of Books*.

I also want to shout out friends and confreres, old and new, whose intellectual and emotional presence and support in my life these past few years has contributed in ways both big and small to the completion of this work. Joshua Yaffa, Kati Marton, Glenn Loury, Jake Lamar, Lauren Collins, Daniel Bergner, and so many others who don't work in the industry but who have deeply impacted me.

Last but not at all least, Tom Mayer—thank you for taking Josh and me out for whiskies that night so that John could see my name on that expense report and ask you if I was working on anything. I don't know how many rounds it will take to make us even for that!